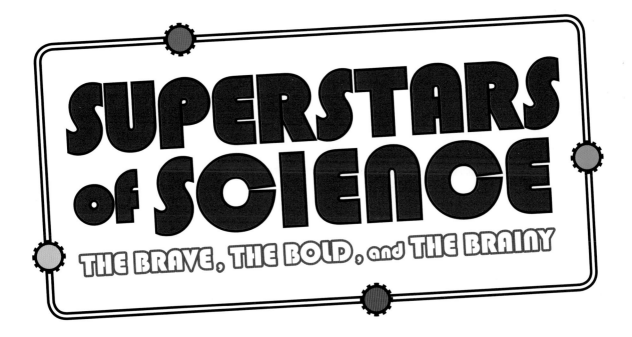

SUPERSTARS of SCIENCE
THE BRAVE, THE BOLD, and THE BRAINY

CREATED BY BASHER ★ WRITTEN BY R.G. GRANT

SCHOLASTIC INC.

Dedicated to Spencer, Katy, and Emmeline Hall

ISBN 978-0-545-82627-3

Created by Basher and Toucan Books Ltd.
Text: R.G. Grant
Consultant: Dr. Kathy Weston
Art Direction: Simon Basher
Editor: Anna Southgate
Designer: Leah Germann
Proofreaders: Marion Dent, Dan Letchworth
Index: Marie Lorimer

Copyright © Toucan Books Ltd/Simon Coleman 2015

12 11 10 9 8 7 6 5 4 3 2 1   15 16 17 18 19 20

Printed in Shenzhen, China
First printing, September 2015

CONTENTS

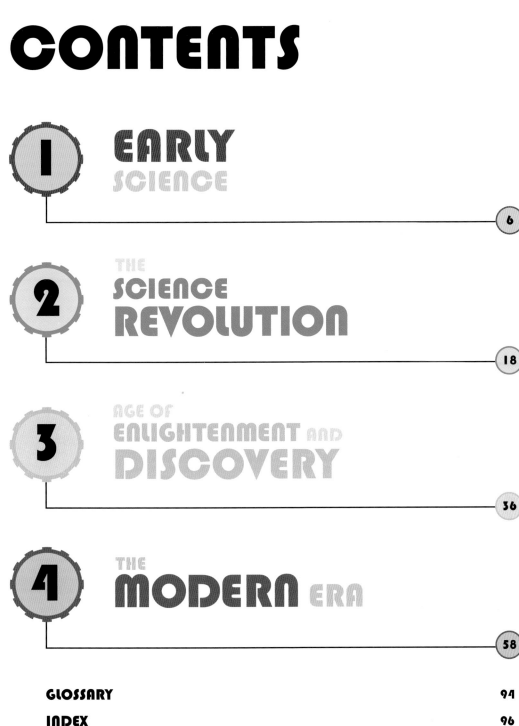

EARLY SCIENCE

1

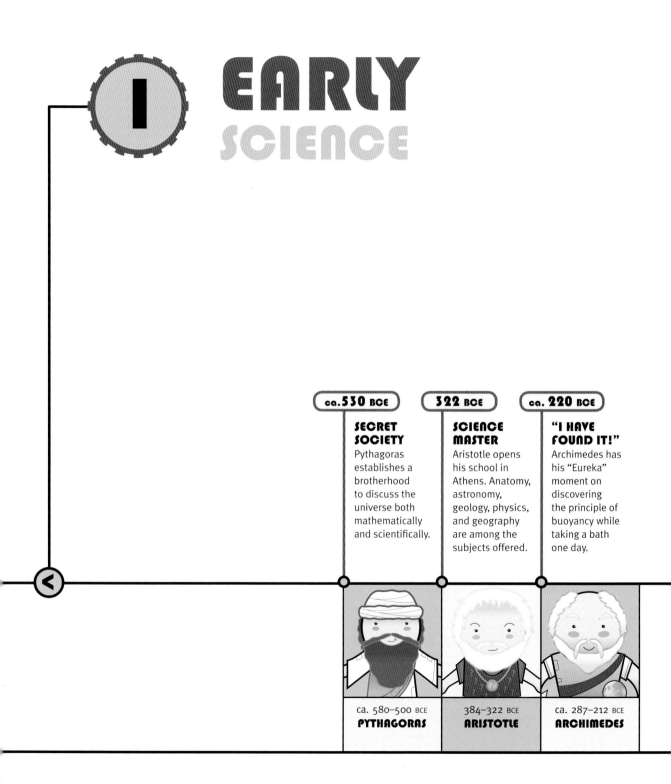

ca. 530 BCE

SECRET SOCIETY

Pythagoras establishes a brotherhood to discuss the universe both mathematically and scientifically.

322 BCE

SCIENCE MASTER

Aristotle opens his school in Athens. Anatomy, astronomy, geology, physics, and geography are among the subjects offered.

ca. 220 BCE

"I HAVE FOUND IT!"

Archimedes has his "Eureka" moment on discovering the principle of buoyancy while taking a bath one day.

ca. 580–500 BCE
PYTHAGORAS

384–322 BCE
ARISTOTLE

ca. 287–212 BCE
ARCHIMEDES

The first scientists were those of ancient civilizations — learned men for whom the mysteries of the earth and everything in it (even beyond it) left too many questions unanswered. Bursting with curiosity, these men wanted to understand the structure of the universe and to explain the physical nature of our planet: How did things move and why? Their work produced many scientific theories and, OK, these early masters didn't always get it right, but they certainly gave future scientists plenty to think about.

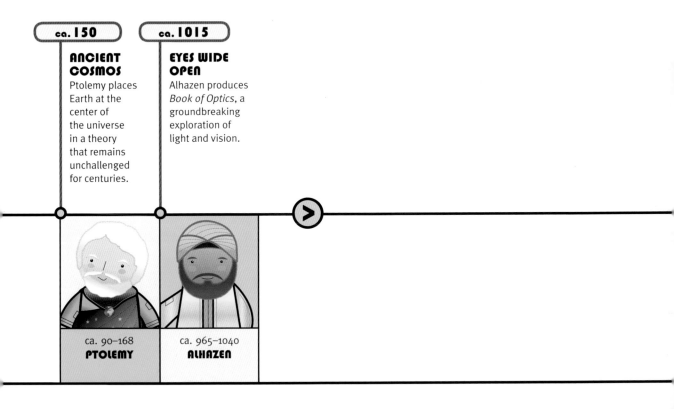

ca. 150

ANCIENT COSMOS

Ptolemy places Earth at the center of the universe in a theory that remains unchallenged for centuries.

ca. 1015

EYES WIDE OPEN

Alhazen produces *Book of Optics*, a groundbreaking exploration of light and vision.

ca. 90–168
PTOLEMY

ca. 965–1040
ALHAZEN

"There is music in the spacing of the spheres."

PYTHAGORAS

In my day nearly everything was a mystery. Greek geeks like me wanted to find the secrets of the universe, but we didn't really know where to look. I traveled around Egypt and farther east to find out what other people thought. I met scholars studying math and wise men watching the stars.

My Secret Brotherhood

When, finally, I felt I had something to teach, I settled down in Italy. I gathered a group of followers called Pythagoreans. Believing our knowledge was too valuable to share, they agreed to keep my wacky ideas to themselves. For example, I believed that people had many lives, their souls shifting after death to other humans or animals. That's why I was vegetarian — who knew whom you might be eating?

Best known for my work with right triangles, I was also fascinated by music. Why was it that some notes were higher or lower? I worked out numbers that related the length of a string to the pitch of the note it produced. If only I could connect these numbers to the movements of the earth and the sun, the planets and the stars, surely I would then be able to uncover the secret of the universe . . .

TIME LINE

ca. 580 BCE Born on the Greek island of Samos

ca. 535 BCE Leaves Samos and begins his travels

ca. 530 BCE Founds the Pythagorean brotherhood at Croton, a Greek colony in southern Italy

ca. 500 BCE Dies at Metapontum, southern Italy

LEGACY

Pythagoras and his followers established the idea of using math to understand the structure of the universe. Like many scientists today, they believed that the ultimate truth of everything might lie in some kind of formula or equation.

GREAT MINDS

The Greek mathematician **Euclid** lived in Alexandria, Egypt, two centuries later than Pythagoras. Known as the father of geometry, he established the basic principles of the discipline. His work was not improved upon for more than 2,000 years, and his methods are still taught in schools today.

PYTHAGOREAN THEOREM

The Pythagoreans gave their name to a mathematical formula (theorem) in geometry. It described an important link between the lengths of the sides of a right triangle. It's one of history's most famous theorems and was used to learn even more about math.

?

What's the story behind the Pythagorean theorem?
It seems that Pythagoras did not discover the right triangle theorem himself (it was already known in India and Babylon). But he or his followers did invent a new and better proof of the theorem.

MUSIC OF THE SPHERES

Pythagoras believed that the universe consisted of a series of spheres around the earth. There was a sphere for the moon, a sphere for the sun, each planet, and so on. As these spheres moved, they generated a sublime but inaudible music that expressed the inner harmony of the universe.

"The study of **every kind of animal** will reveal something **natural** and something **beautiful.**"

ARISTOTLE

No one ever doubted I had brains. But what to do with them? I was born in northern Greece, the son of a doctor. I studied in Athens under the great philosopher Plato, who believed ideas were everything. But thinking wasn't enough for me. I felt you had to look at things up close to really understand them. I set up my own school, the Lyceum, where I developed my philosophy. I taught music, drama, poetry, politics, morality, and psychology, as well as sciences such as astronomy, physics, and zoology.

Striving for Knowledge

Much of what I wrote was little better than guesswork, but it was based on solid facts. I pondered on matters that most people never think about — like, why do things move? Later on, it turned out I got some of the answers wrong, but at least I was asking the right questions.

I was not always popular, though. The people of Athens turned against me and drove me into exile. But that didn't stop me from trying to understand the world. Some even say I drowned myself in the sea, driven to despair because I couldn't explain why there were tides.

TIME LINE

384 BCE Born in Stagira, northern Greece

366 BCE Attends Plato's academy in Athens

335 BCE Opens his own school, the Lyceum, in Athens

322 BCE Dies in exile in Chalcis, on the island of Euboea

OBSERVING NATURE

Aristotle is known to have made careful observations of nature. For example, he broke open chicken eggs to see how a chick developed inside. Yet he was often wrong about humans. He mistakenly thought that intelligence came from the heart and that women had fewer teeth than men.

LEGACY

Aristotle was the first true scientist, because he tried to understand the world by looking at it and not simply by thinking about it. Unfortunately, many of his observations and deductions were plain wrong.

BIG MISTAKES

Aristotle had a great mind, but he wasn't always right. Here are some of his bloopers. He thought that:

* The stars and planets are made from an invisible element called ether (they aren't).
* Heavy objects fall faster than light ones (they don't).
* The earth is the center of the universe (it isn't).

AHEAD OF HIS TIME

★ Aristotle classified plants and animals — from the simplest to the most complex. His system came very close to **theories of evolution** that developed centuries later.

★ He realized that geographical features changed gradually over very long periods of time. His view is confirmed by **modern geology**.

?

Why is Aristotle important?
A thousand years after Aristotle's death, scholars rediscovered his writings. They thought he was a real brainiac and took his ideas as absolute truth. He became the starting point from which all scientists set out — usually to prove him wrong.

"Eureka! I have found it!"

ARCHIMEDES

I was the absent-minded professor type, so caught up in my thoughts that I often failed to notice the world around me. Fellow citizens in Syracuse thought I was odd, and perhaps they were right.

Mathematical Genius

Geometry fascinated me. I was forever drawing diagrams of spheres, cylinders, and spirals. My head was full of strange ideas. I imagined how, with a long enough lever, a man would be able to move Earth just with the power of his arm. I calculated how many grains of sand would fill the universe.

My crazy imaginings and abstract calculations also solved practical problems. I made machines that worked. When the Romans surrounded our city, I masterminded the defense. I built a giant claw that lifted Roman boats approaching the city walls and dashed them on rocks. I used my knowledge of levers to make powerful catapults that spattered the enemy with missiles. But my work always came first. When the Romans finally took the city, I didn't even notice. A Roman soldier broke into my room, but I was deeply absorbed in geometry. He was so annoyed, he stabbed me to death with his sword.

TIME LINE

ca. 287 BCE Born in Syracuse, a Greek city on the island of Sicily

ca. 213 BCE Helps defend Syracuse against a Roman army

ca. 212 BCE Killed when the Romans capture Syracuse

LEGACY

Archimedes was a brilliant Greek mathematician and scientist. He showed how theoretical science could be applied to create practical machines. His fabulous inventions made him famous throughout the ancient world.

GREAT MINDS

Archimedes' only serious rival for the title of "best ancient inventor" was **Hero** (ca. 10–70 CE). A Greek living in Alexandria, Hero made the very first steam engine and the first coin-in-a-slot vending machine — it delivered a cup of holy water.

ARCHIMEDES' MACHINES

Archimedes was a true master of invention.

★ The **Archimedes screw** was a device used for raising water to a higher level by turning a handle.

★ His **odometer** measured how far a cart traveled by automatically dropping a stone in a bucket every mile.

★ His **compound pulley system** was used for lifting heavy weights.

?

And the "Eureka" moment?
Set with the task of telling whether a crown was pure gold, Archimedes knew he had to find its volume. But how? Getting into his bath, he noticed the water rise. What if he put the crown in water? He'd see how much water it would displace, and . . . "Eureka," he shouted, "I have found it!"

THE SAND RECKONER

In his work **The Sand Reckoner**, Archimedes set himself the enormous challenge of figuring out the size of the universe. He wanted to know how many grains of sand it would take to fill it. Through his workings, he invented new numbers to express the huge quantities involved. Even so, he vastly underestimated just how massive the universe is.

"When I follow the **multitude of the stars** in their courses, my feet **no longer touch the earth.**"

PTOLEMY

I was a citizen of Alexandria, a great Greek city in north Africa. Part of the Roman Empire, the city was famous for its library and its learning. Wanting to be the master of everything that was known about Earth, I believed the sun, planets, and stars revolved in circles around it. That our planet stood still while all else had motion seemed obvious. I made charts of the constellations and the movements of heavenly bodies — with considerable accuracy, if I say so myself.

Earth's Mysteries

Sailors told me tales of their travels, from the Canary Islands off the coast of Africa to India and China. I tried to make a scientific world map with longitude and latitude lines to establish where places were in relation to one another. But the sailors had only visited part of the earth, so my map was incomplete.

I believed the earth was round and tried to work out its size. Some 300 years before me another Greek, Eratosthenes, had done this, but my Earth was smaller than his and people believed me. After I died people lost interest in my life story, but my works were respected for centuries.

TIME LINE

ca. 90 CE Born Claudius Ptolemy in Alexandria, Egypt, then part of the Roman Empire

ca. 132–140 CE Makes observations of the stars, planets, and sun

ca. 168 CE Dies in Alexandria

?

Did everyone think that Earth was the center of the universe?
Most people in the ancient world believed this, but not Greek astronomer Aristarchus of Samos (ca. 310–230 BCE). He said the earth revolved around the sun and even guessed the stars were other suns very far away. At the time, everyone thought he was crazy.

LEGACY

Ptolemy was the world's most respected scientist for over one thousand years after his death. His ideas on the stars, the planets, and the earth were almost universally accepted as true — and a few of them turned out to be just that!

PTOLEMY AND COLUMBUS

When explorer Christopher Columbus sailed west from Europe in 1492, he thought he'd reach Asia quickly. This is because he had read Ptolemy's **Geography**. The work told Columbus the world was round, but gave the size of the globe as smaller than it is and the size of Asia as bigger. And, of course, it didn't show America!

PTOLEMY'S BOOKS

Three major works of Ptolemy survived from ancient times:

★ The **Almagest** covered math and astronomy.
★ **Geography** dealt with the earth.
★ **Tetrabiblos** was about astrology — the influence of the stars on people's lives — which Ptolemy regarded as serious science.

GREAT MINDS

In the ancient world, women usually weren't allowed to study science. An exception was **Hypatia**, a Greek mathematician and astronomer living in Alexandria. In 415 CE, she was murdered by a Christian mob, because they rejected her science as godless magic.

"Finding the truth is difficult and the road to it is rough."

ALHAZEN

I was born in the right place at the right time — during the Golden Age of Islamic culture. Every civilization has its day, and ours was probably the most advanced in the world back then.

A Brilliant Mind

I was one of many Muslims inspired by the works of ancient Greek thinkers such as Aristotle and Ptolemy. But I was determined to challenge their writings, to find out the truth of things for myself. I examined the structure of the human eye, experimented with mirrors and prisms, and worked out the reason for rainbows. I pointed out that the stars and planets did not actually move the way Ptolemy's theories suggested.

When I went to Cairo, Caliph al-Hakim, the ruler of Egypt, ordered me to control the annual floods of the Nile River. He had no doubt that a man of my brilliance could do it. But I saw that it would need a dam we simply didn't have the technology to build. The caliph made me a prisoner for ten years. If I hadn't pretended to be insane, he would probably have cut off my head. But I outlived him and went on to complete more than 200 additional works.

TIME LINE

ca. 965 CE Born in Basra, in what is now Iraq

ca. 1011 Arrested in Cairo, Egypt, by Caliph al-Hakim

1021 Released on the death of the caliph

1040 Dies in Cairo

LEGACY

Alhazen's work on optics — studying light, mirrors, and how we see — was an inspiration to later scientists. Even more important were his ideas about how to study science, basing theories on careful observation and experiment.

GREAT MINDS

Leonardo Pisano Fibonacci (ca. 1170–1240), known as Fibonacci, was an Italian mathematician. He introduced many ideas about math that had first been developed by Indian and Arabic scholars to medieval Europe. These included the **"Fibonacci numbers,"** a sequence fundamental to modern math.

KNOWLEDGE TRANSFER

From around 1100, Arabic books were translated into Latin, the language used by Christian European scholars. Through these translations, Europeans discovered Arabic science and many works by the ancient Greeks. This did much to stimulate the flood of new ideas in the arts and sciences that took place in Europe between 1400 and 1600. This period is known as the Renaissance, which means "rebirth."

?

How long was the Islamic Golden Age?

Islamic culture flourished from around 750 to 1300. Alongside advances seen in science and medicine during this time were developments in other disciplines, including the arts, industry, and technology.

SCIENTISTS OF THE ISLAMIC GOLDEN AGE

* **Al-Khwarizmi** (780–850), an outstanding mathematician who developed arithmetic and algebra.

* **Avicenna** (980–1037), best known for his writings on medicine.

* **Averroes** (1126–1198), who carried forward Aristotle's work on astronomy, physics, and philosophy.

2 THE SCIENCE REVOLUTION

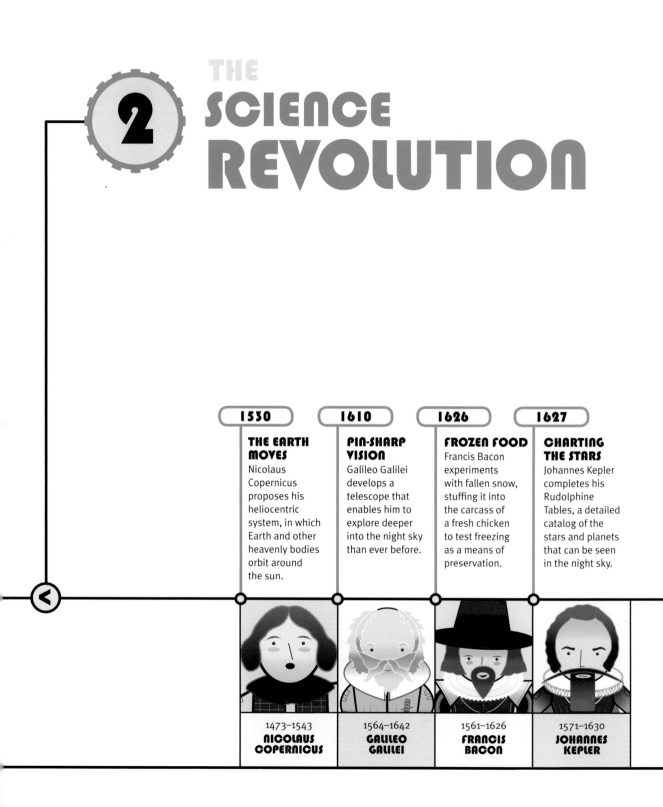

1530

THE EARTH MOVES

Nicolaus Copernicus proposes his heliocentric system, in which Earth and other heavenly bodies orbit around the sun.

1610

PIN-SHARP VISION

Galileo Galilei develops a telescope that enables him to explore deeper into the night sky than ever before.

1626

FROZEN FOOD

Francis Bacon experiments with fallen snow, stuffing it into the carcass of a fresh chicken to test freezing as a means of preservation.

1627

CHARTING THE STARS

Johannes Kepler completes his Rudolphine Tables, a detailed catalog of the stars and planets that can be seen in the night sky.

1473–1543
NICOLAUS COPERNICUS

1564–1642
GALILEO GALILEI

1561–1626
FRANCIS BACON

1571–1630
JOHANNES KEPLER

These heroes were buoyed by the cultural revolution that swept through Europe from the early 1500s. Dubbed the Renaissance (rebirth), this period brought a great thirst for knowledge. The discoveries of this new age challenged the theories of the great ancients for the first time in almost one thousand years. The key to this era's scientific triumphs was "observation." With the invention of the microscope, scientists were able to examine the tiniest things up close, while the telescope revealed the sheer vastness of the night sky.

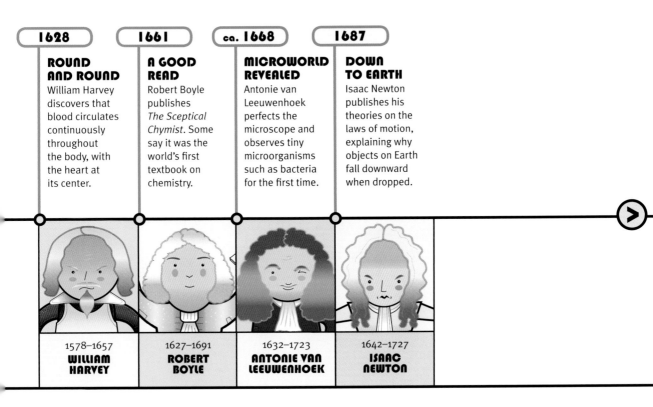

1628

ROUND AND ROUND

William Harvey discovers that blood circulates continuously throughout the body, with the heart at its center.

1578–1657
WILLIAM HARVEY

1661

A GOOD READ

Robert Boyle publishes *The Sceptical Chymist*. Some say it was the world's first textbook on chemistry.

1627–1691
ROBERT BOYLE

ca. 1668

MICROWORLD REVEALED

Antonie van Leeuwenhoek perfects the microscope and observes tiny microorganisms such as bacteria for the first time.

1632–1723
ANTONIE VAN LEEUWENHOEK

1687

DOWN TO EARTH

Isaac Newton publishes his theories on the laws of motion, explaining why objects on Earth fall downward when dropped.

1642–1727
ISAAC NEWTON

"In the **midst of all** dwells the **sun** . . ."

NICOLAUS COPERNICUS

I was the man who made the earth move. Living in a tower by the Baltic Sea in northern Poland, I loved to stare up at the sky on clear nights, observing the planets and the stars. I learned from Aristotle and Ptolemy that the earth was the center of the universe and that everything else revolved around it . . . but something didn't add up.

Rethinking the Universe

While it seemed plain common sense that the earth stood still, the theory didn't match what I saw happening in the night sky. I felt like a blind man stumbling through darkness and then, suddenly, there was light. What if it was the earth that moved around the sun? And what if the planets went around the sun, too? All this spinning made me dizzy, but it also made perfect sense of my nighttime observations. I spent years working on my idea in detail and wrote it all down in a book called *On the Revolutions of the Heavenly Spheres*. But I hesitated to publish it because I feared most people would think I was crazy. By the time the first printed copy of the book arrived, I was already on my deathbed.

LEGACY

Copernicus was an astronomer who rejected the traditional idea that the earth was the center of the universe. By realizing that the earth and planets revolved around the sun, he laid the foundation of modern astronomy.

TIME LINE

1473 Born Niclas Koppernigk in Torun (Thorn), Poland

1491–1503 Studies at universities in Poland and Italy

1542 Completes his book *On the Revolutions of the Heavenly Spheres*

1543 Dies in Frombork (Frauenberg), Poland

GREAT MINDS

Danish astronomer **Tycho Brahe** (1546–1601) studied the stars from an observatory on an island near Copenhagen. His discoveries included showing that comets were bodies traveling in space. But he rejected Copernicus's heliocentric theory, insisting instead that Earth must be the center of the universe.

SUN-CENTERED VISION

The key points of Copernicus's heliocentric (sun-centered) system were:

★ That the sun is the center of the universe.

★ That the moon revolves around the earth, while the earth and all the planets revolve around the sun.

★ That the earth rotates daily on its own axis.

? What happened to Copernicus's book?

Hundreds of copies were printed and circulated among people interested in astronomy. It was controversial because it denied humans' central place in the universe. The Catholic Church banned the book in 1616.

BIG BLUNDER

Copernicus mistakenly accepted the ancient idea that all heavenly bodies — including Earth — must move in perfect circles. He saw the universe as a set of spheres moving in circular orbits, with the sun at the center. It was a step in the right direction but was still far from being correct. It would be almost one hundred years before he was proven wrong.

"All **truths** are easy to **understand** once they are **discovered.**"

GALILEO GALILEI

For a scientist, the era in which I lived was the best of times, but it was also the worst of times. A number of us were just beginning to investigate the world properly — there was so much to discover. But there were powerful people who didn't welcome new knowledge, and that made life dangerous.

Silenced by the Church

Experimentation was my thing. I timed, measured, and calculated everything to work out exactly how things moved. I devised experiments to prove that objects fell at the same speed whether they were light or heavy. My experiments had their uses: I gauged the path of a cannonball so gunners could hit their targets better.

But it was astronomy that did it for me. I made one of the first telescopes and used it to see things that had never been seen before, such as Jupiter's moon and the craters on our moon. I agreed with Copernicus that the earth revolved around the sun. But the Catholic Church didn't like it. The authorities forced me to deny that the earth moved at all! Later, they put me under house arrest and banned my books. And yet I had seen what I had seen, hadn't I?

TIME LINE

1564 Born in Pisa, Italy

1592 Experiments at the University of Padua

1610 Uses a telescope to see the moons of Jupiter

1616 Forced by the Church to deny that the earth moves around the sun

1633 Found guilty of heresy

1642 Dies near Florence, Italy

GREAT MINDS

Galileo was not the only original thinker to fall foul of the Church. Italian **Giordano Bruno** (1548–1600) claimed the sun was a star. He said other stars also had planets that might be inhabited. He was burned at the stake for such heresy.

SCIENCE MATTERS

Galileo's discoveries include finding out:

★ That falling objects accelerate at a fixed rate.

★ That a pendulum can be used to measure time.

★ That a cannonball travels in a type of curve called a parabola.

★ That the planet Jupiter has moons revolving around it.

LEGACY

As a pioneer of experimentation, Galileo is celebrated as a founder of modern science. Building his own telescope, he made new discoveries about the moon and the planets that challenged accepted views of the universe.

LUNAR COUP

Galileo said that in an airless vacuum, a light and a heavy object should fall at the same speed. In 1971, astronaut David Scott dropped a feather and a hammer side by side on the moon. Because the moon is airless, they did indeed land at the same time.

? Why did the Church condemn Galileo?

In the 1600s, the Catholic Church began to worry that new ideas about the universe might undermine religious faith. Galileo's belief that the earth moved around the sun was condemned as heresy (going against Church teaching and the Bible).

a AAAAA
b AAAAB
c AAABA
?

"**Knowledge** *itself is* **power.**"

FRANCIS BACON

Diplomat, politician, lawyer, judge, prisoner in the Tower of London . . . I certainly led a busy life. I won the favor of England's King James I, who knighted me, then made me a lord. He gave me some of the top jobs in the kingdom — Attorney General and Lord Chancellor — and my enemies had me imprisoned for taking bribes. Despite all this, I found time to write on science.

Experimental Bent

In my writings I argued that the only way to understand the world was through observation and experimentation. For me, experiments provided the very best ways to interrogate nature, to force it to reveal its secrets. Most people championed old books — if Aristotle had written something, surely it must be true. But no, I cried, "Books must follow sciences, and not sciences books."

The invention of gunpowder, printing, and the magnetic compass had already transformed the world. If only scientists worked together, deliberately seeking new inventions, I knew progress would be even faster. Obvious, I know, but at the time my ideas were startlingly new.

TIME LINE

1561 Born in London, England

1597 Publishes his first book of essays

1603 Knighted by King James I

1618 Appointed Lord Chancellor

1621 Imprisoned for corruption

1626 Dies in London

LEGACY

Bacon has been called the father of experimental science. He firmly established the principle that scientists should seek the truth through experiment and observation and then apply their knowledge to practical inventions.

BACON'S CIPHER

Bacon was often involved in handling state secrets. He invented a code, called **Bacon's cipher**, for sending messages hidden in apparently innocent documents. It was a binary code — incredibly, the same kind of code now used in computer programs.

MARTYR TO SCIENCE

Bacon is said to have died as the result of a scientific experiment. He stuffed a chicken carcass with snow to see whether freezing would preserve the meat. Handling the snow gave him a chill and he caught a fever. Bacon died of pneumonia a few days later. The experiment worked, though, preserving the meat for several days.

?

Did Bacon write Shakespeare's plays?
Some people believe that Bacon wrote many of the plays attributed to English playwright William Shakespeare, who was alive at the same time. Their main argument is that Bacon was the only man brilliant enough to have written such great plays. But there is no direct evidence to support the theory.

THE NEW ATLANTIS

At the time of his death, Francis Bacon was writing a fantasy novel called *The New Atlantis*. In it, Bacon described an imaginary Pacific island on which scientists worked in a research institute. The institute was called Salomon's House and was financed by the island's king. It became the model for England's world-famous Royal Society, founded in 1660.

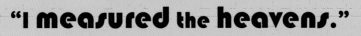

"I measured the heavens."

JOHANNES KEPLER

In my day no one knew the difference between math and magic, science and witchcraft. I worked alongside alchemists who tried to turn ordinary metals into gold. My bosses paid me as an astrologer, using my knowledge of the stars to predict the future. Well, who knew what was true or false?

Mapping the Skies

I was sure Copernicus was right to say the earth moved around the sun. I worked out the exact movements of the planets for myself and discovered that they went in ellipses, not circles, as had always been believed. I was even able to describe their movements precisely using math, which was brilliant.

But I lived in difficult times. In Europe, Catholics and Protestants were at war. I was a Protestant who worked for Catholic emperors and princes, so I had to watch my step. Nevertheless, I kept working at my star charts, the Rudolphine Tables. As long as people believed the stars ruled their lives, this was essential knowledge and I was prized for it. For myself, the cosmos remained a mystery, but I reckoned math might one day unlock its secrets.

TIME LINE

1571 Born in Weil der Stadt, southern Germany

1601 Becomes court astronomer to Emperor Rudolph II in Prague

1609 Publishes *New Astronomy*

1627 Completes the Rudolphine Tables, detailed star charts

1630 Dies in Regensburg, Germany

SCIENCE FIRSTS

★ In his book *New Astronomy*, Kepler described the planets moving in ellipses, not circles.

★ His Rudolphine Tables charted the past, present, and future positions of more than 1,000 stars and the planets.

★ His work on optics included the first correct description of how the lens in the human eye functions.

LEGACY

A mathematician and astronomer, Kepler played a major role in the seventeenth-century scientific revolution. His three laws of planetary motion challenged long-accepted views, setting man's understanding of the universe in a new direction.

TRANSIT OF MERCURY

In 1629, just before his death, Kepler predicted that the planet Mercury would pass between Earth and the sun in November 1631. This **"transit of Mercury"** was successfully observed by French astronomer **Pierre Gassendi**, confirming Kepler's theories.

QUIRKY KEPLER

✷ Kepler's mother, Katharina, was found guilty of witchcraft. Her son fought a legal battle to have her freed from prison.

✷ Kepler's writings included advice on the optimal way to pack round objects, such as oranges on a fruit stall.

✷ He was the first person to question the six-cornered geometry of a snowflake.

?

Was Kepler the first sci-fi writer?
Some might argue that Kepler invented science fiction. His book *Somnium (The Dream)*, written in 1608, recounts a journey to the moon. It describes the earth and other planets seen from the moon's surface and tells tales of the monsters who live there.

"I profess to **learn** . . . **not from books**
but from **dissections.**"

WILLIAM HARVEY

An ultra-successful physician, I was entrusted with the health of the English monarchy, but what really interested me was cutting things up. I went to medical school at Padua, in Italy, where they'd been dissecting bodies for years.

The Motion of Blood

I wanted to see how the body actually worked, and for that I needed to cut up the living, not the dead. Well, you just couldn't do that with people, so I operated on live animals instead. I saw how their hearts beat and how the blood traveled along their veins and arteries. I tied up these tubes to see what happened if the blood flow was stopped. My experiments showed that the heart pumped blood around the body. The arteries carried blood away from the heart, while the veins brought it back. My discoveries were revolutionary and I wrote them all down in my book *An Anatomical Exercise on the Motion of the Heart and Blood in Living Beings*.

Later, I tried to find the secret of generation — how animals actually got made. I had some ideas, of course, but without a microscope (not yet invented), I must confess, I was stumped.

TIME LINE

1578 Born in Folkestone, Kent, England

1599–1602 Studies medicine at the University of Padua

1618 Appointed doctor to King James I

1628 Publishes his book on the circulation of the blood

1651 Publishes *On the Generation of Animals*

1657 Dies in London, England

LEGACY

William Harvey is the father of modern physiology, the science that explores bodily functions. His work on circulation was a major advancement in medical science, overturning beliefs that had been accepted as fact for more than one thousand years.

GREAT MINDS

The ancient Greek physician **Hippocrates** of Cos (ca. 460–370 BCE) is known as the "father of medicine." He established that illness could be explained as the result of all sorts of natural causes rather than being a punishment of the gods. He introduced the Hippocratic Oath, binding physicians to maintain high moral standards.

IN THE FAMILY

Harvey certainly wasn't the squeamish type. It is said that he dissected the deceased corpses of both his father and his sister. Since bodies for dissection were very hard to come by, he presumably saw their deaths as too good an opportunity to miss.

?

Do people still operate on animals?
Yes, they do. In Harvey's day, scientists dissected many different types of living things in order to learn about the workings of the human body. Today, such practices are used only where no other means exist. In such cases, surgery is strictly controlled.

THE HUMAN FABRIC

In 1543, Belgian physician **Andreas Vesalius** (1514–1564) published an illustrated book showing human bodies that he had dissected at the University of Padua. The detailed images of bones, muscles, inner organs, veins, and arteries revolutionized knowledge of human anatomy.

"I study the **book** of **nature**."

ROBERT BOYLE

I was born into the aristocracy — the son of the Earl of Cork — so earning a living was never a problem for me. Instead, I spent my time on the two things that I loved the most — scientific experiments and thoughts about religion. Along with several other British thinkers and experimenters, I formed "the invisible college," a society that delved into the nature of the universe.

The Royal Society

Chemistry was my thing. I decided that matter must consist of particles too small to see and that the movement of these particles explained most things. It was through experiments with an air pump I'd built that I came to formulate a law all about pressure. Of course, it came to be known as Boyle's Law. What a gas!

In 1660, our little college gained the support of the king and became known as the Royal Society. I was one of its foremost members. I studied many things — color and light, heat and cold, how creatures breathe, how sound travels, and more. In later years, I spent much of my money funding Christian missionary work overseas.

TIME LINE

1627 Born at Lismore Castle, County Waterford, Ireland

1661 Publishes his book *The Sceptical Chymist*

1662 States Boyle's Law

1660 Is a founding member of the Royal Society

1691 Dies in London, England

BOYLE'S LAW IN ACTION

According to Boyle's Law, the more gas you have in a given space, the greater the pressure it exerts. You can see this when pumping up a tire. Forcing more air into the space inside the tire increases the pressure, making the tire firm. Eventually the pressure would grow so great, the tire would burst.

LEGACY

The founder of modern chemistry, Robert Boyle is best known for his law on the pressure of gases. In helping to set up the Royal Society, Boyle pioneered a systematic approach to experiments and enabled the spread of scientific knowledge.

WISH LIST

In 1662, Boyle wrote a wish list of twenty-four desirable inventions, many of which are now a reality. They included:

* Perpetual light.
* The art of flying.
* Making armor light and extremely hard.
* Having a ship that didn't depend on the wind.

SMART SISTER

For twenty-three years, Boyle shared a house with his sister Katherine, Viscountess Ranelagh. She was his equal in intelligence, and they carried out many experiments together, though he took the credit. They both died in the same week in December 1691.

?

Was Boyle English or Irish?
Boyle's father was an Englishman who owned land in Ireland. Boyle lived most of his life in England, but he was born in Ireland and could speak the native Irish language. So he had at least a bit of the shamrock in him.

"My work . . . was not pursued in order to gain praise . . . but chiefly from a **craving** after **knowledge.**"

ANTONIE VAN
LEEUWENHOEK

Living in the small Dutch town of Delft, I was just an ordinary guy — a successful businessman who was prosperous, reliable, and respected in the local community. I was definitely not the sort you'd see making great scientific discoveries. And yet that is exactly what I did when I entered a world no one even knew existed — the world of the ultrasmall.

Microscopic Vision

There was nothing new about the microscope, that's for sure, but my secret was the ability to make microscopes that magnified twenty times more than anyone else's. They were tiny — just a couple of inches long — and not at all easy to use, but what surprises there were! Did you know that every drop of water you drink contains masses of living creatures invisible to the naked eye? You do now!

When I wrote to the scientists at London's Royal Society about my discoveries, they wouldn't believe me. They knew me, and had liked my ideas so far, so I invited them to see for themselves. Of course, once they'd used my microscope, they could doubt me no longer. I became famous, but carried happily on with my observations almost until the day I died.

TIME LINE

1632 Born in Delft, in the Netherlands

ca. 1668 Begins observations with microscopes

1673 First writes to the Royal Society in London, reporting his discoveries

1680 Elected a member of the Royal Society

1723 Dies in Delft

LEGACY

Leeuwenhoek (pronounced lay-van-hook) was the first biologist to study microscopic organisms. In doing so, he discovered the existence of bacteria. The microscope he invented suddenly made the tiniest cells visible to the human eye.

GREAT MINDS

English scientist **Robert Hooke** (1635–1703) published a book called *Micrographia* in 1665. It had spectacular illustrations of what Hooke had seen through a microscope — for example, the structure of a fly's eye. A bestseller, the book may have inspired Leeuwenhoek.

LEEUWENHOEK'S LENSES

During the 1600s, most microscopes magnified an object up to thirty times. By polishing and grinding his lenses more precisely, Leeuwenhoek magnified objects to several hundred times their actual size. His lenses were not bettered until the 1800s.

?

How does a microscope work?
First seen in the 1590s, a typical microscope uses two or more curved glass lenses placed in a tube. When you observe an object through the microscope, the lenses bend the light that passes through in such a way that it magnifies the object under observation.

MICRO-FINDINGS

Among Leeuwenhoek's major triumphs were:

★ The discovery of bacteria in the plaque around teeth.

★ Finding that blood was composed of cells.

★ Discovering spermatozoa (*sperm* for short) and how they fertilized eggs.

★ Identifying the tiny creatures found living in pond water.

"My greatest friend is truth."

ISAAC NEWTON

Something of a loner, I never married and did not always get along with my friends. But when it came to thinking, no one could match me. I would concentrate so hard that I often forgot to eat!

One day, while sitting in my garden, I watched an apple fall from a tree. Suddenly everything made sense. I realized that the force holding the planets in orbit around the sun must be the same as the force that made apples fall to the ground on Earth. This force was gravity. I didn't really understand how it worked, but I did a lot of complicated math that showed it must be true.

A Questioning Mind
I invented a reflecting telescope that worked with a mirror instead of a lens, and experimented with prisms, but mostly I was an ideas man. After I published my work on the laws of motion, *Principia Mathematica,* people hailed me as the founder of the Age of Reason. But I wasn't so sure. I dabbled in alchemy and spent years trying to use the Bible to determine when the world would end (2060 could be about right). At heart, the universe remained a mystery to me.

TIME LINE

1642 Born in Lincolnshire, England

1665–66 Makes breakthrough discovery about gravity

1668 Demonstrates his reflecting telescope

1687 Publishes *Principia Mathematica*

1703 Elected president of the Royal Society

1704 Publishes *Opticks,* a book on light

1727 Dies in London, England

VORTEX SCHMORTEX

René Descartes (1596–1650) was the French philosopher who said: "I think, therefore I am." He was also a scientist. He came up with a theory that the planets were moved by swirling "vortices," like whirlpools in water. Newton dismissed this as plain silly.

NEWTON'S GREATEST HITS

★ Newton explained the movement of planets and of falling bodies on Earth through gravity.

★ He stated the three laws of motion.

★ He showed that white light contains the colors of the rainbow.

★ He founded the branch of math called calculus.

LEGACY

Isaac Newton may have been the greatest scientist ever. His laws of motion explained the movement of the planets and why objects on Earth fall downward. He made other major discoveries in math and in the understanding of light.

ACTION AND REACTION

Newton's third law of motion states that every action produces an equal and opposite reaction. This is the principle that makes a jet or rocket engine work. Firing gas backward makes an aircraft or spacecraft go forward.

?

Was Newton inspired by an apple falling on his head?
The famous story of the apple is mostly true. Newton often said the idea of gravity came to him when he was sitting in a garden and saw an apple fall. But it didn't fall on his head — that bit was made up.

AGE OF ENLIGHTENMENT AND DISCOVERY

3

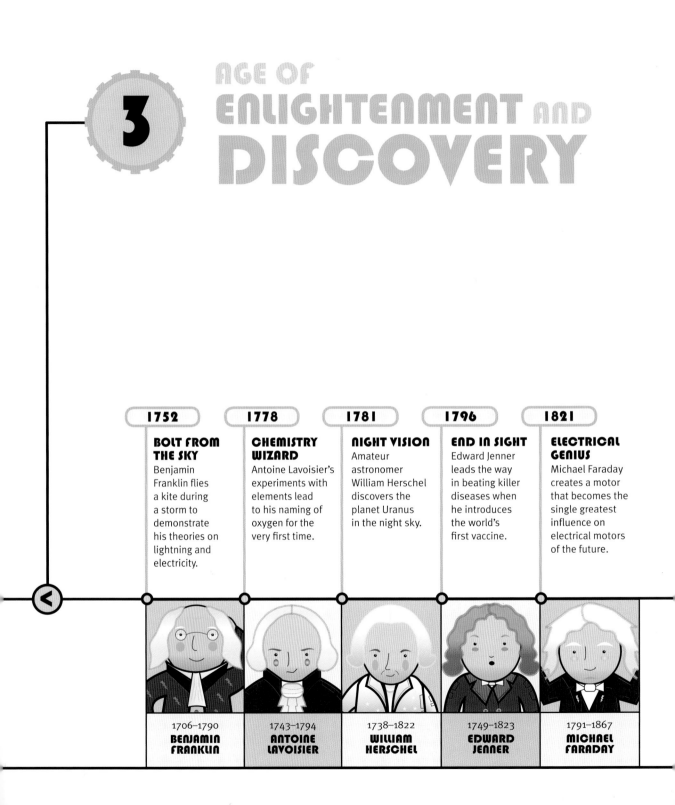

1752

BOLT FROM THE SKY

Benjamin Franklin flies a kite during a storm to demonstrate his theories on lightning and electricity.

1778

CHEMISTRY WIZARD

Antoine Lavoisier's experiments with elements lead to his naming of oxygen for the very first time.

1781

NIGHT VISION

Amateur astronomer William Herschel discovers the planet Uranus in the night sky.

1796

END IN SIGHT

Edward Jenner leads the way in beating killer diseases when he introduces the world's first vaccine.

1821

ELECTRICAL GENIUS

Michael Faraday creates a motor that becomes the single greatest influence on electrical motors of the future.

1706–1790
BENJAMIN FRANKLIN

1743–1794
ANTOINE LAVOISIER

1738–1822
WILLIAM HERSCHEL

1749–1823
EDWARD JENNER

1791–1867
MICHAEL FARADAY

By the 1750s, there were several institutions dedicated to scientific discovery. Here, inquisitive men and women developed theories and launched experiments in medicine, astronomy, chemistry, physics, botany, and more. As they did so, they laid the foundations of modern science. These are the heroes who first experimented with electricity and the chemical elements that make up our planet, who developed groundbreaking ways to fight disease, and who began to understand, for the very first time, that there are scientific reasons for each of us looking just like mom and dad.

1824
FOSSIL FIND
Fossil expert Mary Anning finds the first complete plesiosaurus skeleton in the Jurassic rocks of Lyme Regis, England.

1843
COMPUTER PROPHET
Visionary Ada Lovelace writes the world's first-ever computer program, preempting the digital age by about one hundred years.

1854
PEAS IN A POD
Gregor Mendel starts experiments with pea plants that lead to his theories about the passing on of characteristics from generation to generation.

1859
SURVIVAL OF THE FITTEST
Charles Darwin's book *On the Origin of Species* explains his controversial theories on evolution.

ca. 1860
MICRO DISCOVERY
Through his microscopic experiments, Louis Pasteur proves that germs cause disease and infection.

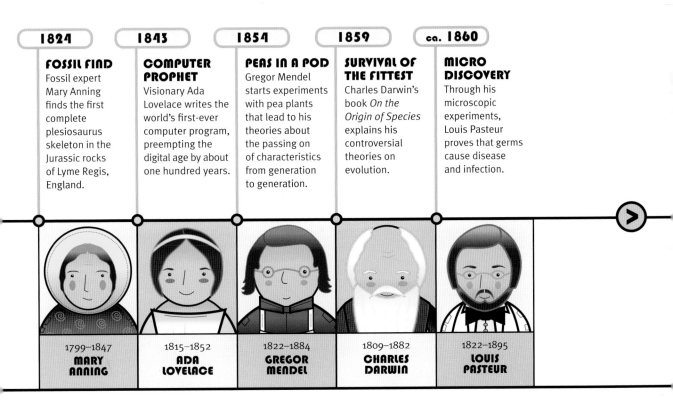

1799–1847	1815–1852	1822–1884	1809–1882	1822–1895
MARY ANNING	**ADA LOVELACE**	**GREGOR MENDEL**	**CHARLES DARWIN**	**LOUIS PASTEUR**

"Tell me and I **forget**. Teach me and I **remember**. Involve me and I **learn**."

BENJAMIN FRANKLIN

A natural businessman, I left school at ten and made my fortune by the age of forty. My many achievements during a busy life include running the postal service and helping found the United States of America. I was also a scientist.

Incredibly curious, I read about experiments exploring electricity and made the brilliant guess that lightning was electrical. I tested my theory by flying a kite in stormy weather. Sure enough, sparks flew when electricity flowed down the wet kite string to a key I'd attached at the bottom. My ideas about electricity put me at the forefront of science.

I realized correctly that positive and negative electricity were different aspects of the same thing, not two different fluids, as some claimed.

For the Good of All

My belief that knowledge should be useful and practically applied led me to invent many things, including the metal lightning rod. Placed atop a building and connected to the ground by a wire, it stopped the building from being struck by lightning during a storm. First installed at the Academy of Philadelphia, it was a strike of pure genius!

TIME LINE

1706 Born in Boston, Massachusetts

1723 Moves to Philadelphia, aged seventeen

1752 Demonstrates that lightning is electricity

1776 Helps draw up the Declaration of Independence

1783 Signs the Treaty of Paris, ending the American Revolutionary War

1790 Dies in Philadelphia, Pennsylvania

LEGACY

A Founding Father of the United States, Benjamin Franklin was also an influential scientist who made important advances in the understanding of electricity. He pioneered the use of science for finding ways of improving day-to-day living.

SCIENTIFIC GENEROSITY

Franklin refused to patent any of his inventions, which would mean that only he could profit from them. Instead, he made his inventions available to everyone without charge. He wrote that "we should be glad of an opportunity to serve others by any invention of ours; and this we should do freely and generously."

CHARTING THE OCEAN

Franklin was the first person to chart the course of the Gulf Stream, the warm ocean current off North America's eastern seaboard. He created his chart, published in 1770, from evidence provided by experienced sea captains who had sailed the Atlantic.

? Did Franklin really fly a kite in a thunderstorm?

Franklin was a sensible man. He didn't fly his kite amid thunder and lightning, but toward storm clouds. German scientist **Georg Richmann** was killed by lightning when he carried out electrical experiments during a thunderstorm in 1753.

EVER THE INVENTOR

Benjamin Franklin's various inventions included:

★ **Swim fins** — oval, handheld pieces of wood that made for faster swimming.

★ The **Franklin stove**, a fireplace that produced more heat and less smoke.

★ **Bifocal eyeglasses**, for people who were near- and far-sighted.

"Nothing is **lost**, nothing is **created**, everything is **transformed**."

ANTOINE LAVOISIER

For me, life was a gas . . . until I lost my head, that is. Born into a wealthy French elite that believed in improving the world through knowledge and brainpower, I worked for the government, but devoted my spare time to chemistry.

I experimented with metals, igniting them and observing what happened to them and the air around them as they burned. I showed that the metal became heavier, not lighter, as some scientists had suggested . . . something was added to the metal, not lost. This "something" was a gas in the air, which I called oxygen. I went on to discover that the gases hydrogen and oxygen joined together to form water.

Revolutionary Events
I had found that "elements," such as iron or hydrogen, were unchanging, but that they combined to make up more complex substances. I explained this revolutionary view in my *Elementary Treatise on Chemistry* in 1789. Unhappily for me, another kind of revolution was underway — the French Revolution. Sadly, those revolutionaries weren't interested in my science. All they could see in me was a rich enemy of the people, and they cut off my head.

TIME LINE

1743 Born in Paris, France

1768 Elected to the French Academy of Sciences

1777 Identifies the role of oxygen in burning (combustion)

1789 Publishes his *Elementary Treatise on Chemistry*

1794 Executed by guillotine in Paris

BESIDES CHEMISTRY

Lavoisier was more than just a chemist. He also:
- Helped create a geological map of France.
- Improved the quality of the gunpowder in the royal arsenal.
- Helped invent the metric system of measurement.

LEGACY

Regarded as the father of modern chemistry, Lavoisier is best known for discovering the part played by oxygen in combustion. His *Elementary Treatise on Chemistry* is considered by many to be the first modern textbook on chemistry.

THE CHEMICAL REVOLUTION

Other scientists who contributed to modern chemistry include:

✳ **Joseph Black** (1728–1799), who discovered carbon dioxide in air.
✳ **Joseph Priestley** (1733–1804), who discovered oxygen before Lavoisier.
✳ **John Dalton** (1766–1844), who said that chemical elements were made of small particles called atoms.

?
Why was Lavoisier executed?
Lavoisier worked for the French king as a "tax farmer," collecting taxes and taking a profit. Tax farmers were very unpopular. Once the revolution got rid of the king, all former tax farmers were arrested. A revolutionary court sentenced Lavoisier to the guillotine.

BREATHING AND BURNING

Lavoisier carried out experiments on guinea pigs, measuring the gases they breathed in and out and the heat they generated. He concluded that respiration had the same effect on air as a candle flame — that it was a slow form of burning.

"I have looked **further into space** than ever **human did before me.**"

WILLIAM HERSCHEL

Obsessed with astronomy, I made my own telescopes and set them up in my garden. When the sky was clear at night — not always the case in England — I marveled at what I could see. I taught my eye to pick out faint clouds of gas (nebulae) and clusters of connected stars, carefully charting their positions.

A Stroke of Luck

One night, I spotted an object that was neither a comet nor a star, but a previously unknown planet. I called it George's Star, after Britain's ruler, George III, but other scientists preferred Uranus (after a Greek god) and eventually that stuck. Still, the discovery made me famous and I became King's Astronomer. Devoting all my time to surveying the night sky, I built the biggest telescope in the world.

Yet, however many nebulae and star clusters I charted, I could never be sure what I was looking at. I guessed I might be witnessing galaxies beyond our own and stars being born and dying over vast periods of time at incredible distances from Earth. But the truth would have to wait for an astronomer with an even better telescope than mine.

TIME LINE

1738 Born in Hanover, Germany

1757 Moves to England

1773 Begins observing the planets and stars

1781 Discovers a new planet, Uranus

1785 Builds a giant, forty-foot (twelve-meter) telescope

1822 Dies in Slough, England

LEGACY

William Herschel gained fame for discovering the planet Uranus, but there was more. The large telescopes he built enabled him to explore deep space and to suggest that the universe was bigger and older than people had ever imagined.

SISTER SCIENTIST

William Herschel's sister, Caroline (1750–1848), worked alongside him. At first he treated her as his assistant, but she came to be recognized as a leading astronomer in her own right. She discovered eight new comets and published a famous catalog of stars.

MUSIC TO THE EARS

Herschel came from a musical family and built up a career as a composer and performer before becoming famous as an astronomer. He composed twenty-four symphonies and fourteen concertos. He also appeared in many concerts, performing music on the oboe, the violin, the harpsichord, and the organ.

?

Did Herschel believe in aliens?

Herschel believed in extraterrestrial life. He thought there were living beings not only on the moon and on Mars, but also on unknown planets in distant galaxies. He even once wrote that there might be intelligent creatures living inside the sun!

HERSCHEL'S ASTRONOMICAL DISCOVERIES

★ The planet Uranus.

★ Two moons of Saturn and two of Uranus.

★ As many as 3,500 nebulae and star clusters.

★ Seasonal changes in the polar ice caps on Mars.

★ Infrared radiation, a form of energy he found while carrying out experiments with prisms.

"I hope that **some day** . . .
there will be **no more smallpox**."

EDWARD JENNER

In my day, smallpox was one of the world's most feared diseases. It spread like wildfire, covering victims in gruesome blisters. Many died, and survivors were left disfigured by pockmarks or even blinded. Smallpox was a BIG problem! The only way to prevent the disease was by injecting patients with smallpox! But this had very unpleasant effects and could even be fatal.

Introducing My Vaccine
An English country doctor, I noticed that local dairymaids, didn't catch smallpox. Instead, they picked up cowpox — a much milder disease passed on from the cows they milked. I tried infecting eight-year-old James Phipps, my gardener's son, with cowpox. Then I injected him with smallpox. Miraculously, he had no reaction to it. The boy had been immunized.

I made my discovery public, but was ridiculed. Injection with cowpox might give you the head of a cow, my mockers claimed. But soon my success was obvious and I was hailed a savior. Mounting mass vaccination campaigns, I realized if enough people were vaccinated, the disease would die out. And, in time, it did.

TIME LINE

1749 Born in Berkeley, England

1796 Vaccinates a small boy with cowpox

1798 Publishes the results of his experiments with "vaccine"

1803 Founds a society to promote vaccination

1823 Dies in Berkeley, England

GREAT MINDS

As wife to the British ambassador of Turkey in 1717, **Lady Mary Wortley Montagu** (1689–1762) witnessed the Asian practice of inoculation against smallpox. Back in Britain, she campaigned for inoculation. As a result many people had their children inoculated, before Jenner's safer method took over.

LEGACY

English physician Edward Jenner pioneered vaccination as a way of preventing smallpox, a killer disease that claimed hundreds of thousands of lives each year. His work inspired all future mass immunization campaigns.

THE SCIENCE EXPLAINED

★ **Inoculation** was the method used to combat smallpox before Jenner. It involved deliberately infecting a person with a mild dose of smallpox.

★ **Vaccination** was the name Jenner gave to his method of infecting a person with cowpox "vaccine." It gave immunity to smallpox at lower risk.

CUCKOO OR WHAT?

A keen naturalist, Jenner was the first person to study the habits of the cuckoo, a bird that lays its eggs in other birds' nests. Bizarrely enough, he was made a fellow of the famous Royal Society in London for his cuckoo studies — not for his groundbreaking work on smallpox.

?
What happened to smallpox?
In 1853, the British Parliament ruled that every child must be vaccinated against smallpox. Mass vaccination campaigns gradually spread across the world. In 1980, the World Health Organization declared that smallpox had been eradicated from the world.

"**Nothing** is too **wonderful** to be **true** if it be consistent with the **laws of nature.**"

MICHAEL FARADAY

An unlikely scientist, I had poor parents and little education, yet science fascinated me. Working as an assistant to the famous scientist Sir Humphry Davy at London's Royal Institution, I found time for my own experiments in a basement laboratory.

An Innate Dynamism

The buzzword at the time (quite literally) was *electricity*, and my investigations suggested the world was stranger than anyone had ever thought. I guessed that electricity and magnetism exerted invisible force fields. I found out that magnets affect light — how weird is that? And using just a magnet, an iron ring, and a few pieces of copper wire, I managed to make an electric motor and a generator.

Something of a live wire myself, I had a true gift for inspiring others with the enthusiasm I felt about my work. My lectures at the Royal Institution sold out. The government employed me to improve its lighthouses and I was one of the first antipollution campaigners. I became a famous public figure, but I never lost touch with my humble roots. I turned down a knighthood and refused a burial plot in Westminster Abbey, instead going to a simple grave.

TIME LINE

1791 Born in London, England

1813 Becomes a chemical assistant at the Royal Institution

1821 Makes a primitive electric motor

1825 Begins popular lectures at the Royal Institution

1831 Creates first electrical generator

1867 Dies in London, England

LEGACY

British chemist and physicist Michael Faraday was a successful popularizer of scientific knowledge. He made giant strides in the understanding of electricity, his work laying the ground for the widespread practical use of electric power.

INSTITUTIONAL VALUES

The **Royal Institution**, where Faraday did most of his work, was founded in London in 1799. It was dedicated to spreading scientific knowledge and applying science to improving everyday life. The Institution's famous **Christmas Lectures**, started by Faraday, continue today.

ELECTRIFYING PERSONALITIES

* **Luigi Galvani** (1737–1798) discovered that electricity made the muscle in a frog's leg twitch.
* **Alessandro Volta** (1745–1827) invented the world's first electrical battery.
* **James Clerk Maxwell** (1831–1879) developed Faraday's theories on electric and magnetic force fields.

?

Did Faraday invent the electric motor?
Yes, he did. Others followed him, developing electric motors that could be used with machinery. They include the British scientist **William Sturgeon** (in 1832) and the German engineer **Moritz von Jacobi** (in 1834).

FARADAY'S SCIENCE

★ He discovered electromagnetic induction — the principle behind transformers and generators.

★ He discovered electromagnetic rotation — the principle behind electric motors.

★ He proposed fields of force created by electricity and magnetism.

★ He developed an early form of Bunsen burner.

"[She] has won a **name for herself** and deserves to **win it.**" (Charles Dickens)

MARY ANNING

No one ever called me a scientist. I was a woman, for starters, and women were not taken all that seriously at the time. I grew up living in poverty, and that never helps, either. Yet I reckon I knew more about fossils than any other person alive.

I lived by the sea in Lyme Regis, where I was able to make a little money selling fossils — they were common in the local cliffs there. When I was twelve, my brother and I found a large skeleton, which we sold for good money. Scientists called it an ichthyosaur and put it on display in London. Imagine!

Prehistoric Life Revealed

I soon became an expert, not just in collecting fossils, but in interpreting what I found. I opened a shop that became famous with fossil collectors. Geologists consulted me, because I understood fossils better than any professor.

Gradually, my work changed accepted views of the past. I made scientists see that our planet was older than had ever been thought, and that many creatures once lived on Earth but no longer existed. And still I died without being recognized as a scientist, which, surely I should have been.

TIME LINE

1799 Born in Lyme Regis, Dorset, England

1811 Finds ichthyosaur skeleton

1823 Finds first complete plesiosaur

1826 Opens shop selling fossils in Lyme Regis

1847 Dies in Lyme Regis, England

THE SCOOP ON POOP

Anning demonstrated her skill as a scientist through her study of the small fossils known at the time as "bezoar stones." By examining where they were found and what they contained, she proved that they were the fossilized feces (that's poo to you) of ichthyosaurs and plesiosaurs. Today, scientists call these stony poop samples coprolites.

LEGACY

Mary Anning's collection and study of fossils in the south of England laid the foundation for a revolutionary new understanding of prehistoric life. Sadly, her contribution to science was not properly recognized in her lifetime.

FOSSIL FINDS

Anning's most spectacular fossil discoveries were skeletons of giant reptiles — ichthyosaurs and plesiosaurs. These creatures had lived in the seas of the Triassic era, between 250 and 90 million years ago. Anning also discovered the skeleton of a pterosaur, a large flying reptile.

ESCAPING DEATH

* In August 1800, as a baby, Anning was with three women when lightning struck. All three women were killed, but Anning miraculously survived.
* In October 1833, searching for fossils, Anning narrowly escaped a cliff fall that killed her beloved black-and-white dog, Tray.

? Did Mary Anning discover dinosaurs?

The large fossils Anning found were not dinosaurs, but giant reptiles. The first dinosaur known to science was *Megalosaurus*, described by geologist **William Buckland** in 1824. This dinosaur's bones came from a lime quarry in Oxfordshire, central England.

"That **brain** of mine is something **more than merely mortal.**"

ADA LOVELACE

My parents were messed-up celebrities who split up the moment I appeared. My dad was Lord Byron, a poet famous for being mad and bad. Mom had me educated in math and science — very unusual for a girl in my time — so I wouldn't develop Dad's poetic madness. Well, I still got myself wrapped up in more than a few scandals, but I did turn out to be especially good at math.

Computer Whiz

I was eighteen when I met Charles Babbage, who was working on machines that could make calculations. I loved his idea for an Analytical Engine, a computer that could be programmed using punched cards. Charles saw the machine as a way of performing mathematical operations. But I could see that it had potential to do so much more. I wrote an algorithm — a set of instructions to program his computer. I explained to Charles how such a machine could do anything he wanted, as long as he expressed the instructions in numbers. Sadly, Charles never actually managed to build his machine! And me? I was often ill and I died young, but I had foreseen the digital information age.

TIME LINE

1815 Born in London, England

1833 Becomes interested in Babbage's computer experiments

1830 Meets her mentor, Mary Somerville

1843 Writes a computer program for the Analytical Engine

1852 Dies in London, England

LEGACY

Ada Lovelace is celebrated as a prophet of the computer age. She foresaw the vast potential of computers a century before they became a practical reality. Lovelace is credited with writing the first-ever computer program.

A COMPUTER OF SORTS

In the 1800s, the nearest thing to a real computer was a machine designed by **Herman Hollerith** (1860–1929), used for processing the information from the 1890 US Census. Data was entered using punched cards and the machine churned out the census results in record time.

BABBAGE'S AMAZING MACHINES

English mathematician **Charles Babbage** (1791–1871) is famous for machines he never built. He spent twenty years on a calculating machine, the **Difference Engine**, which he never finished. He then planned the **Analytical Engine**, a programmable computer, but he never finished that either!

?

What is Ada Lovelace Day?
Ada Lovelace Day is an international celebration of the achievements of women — past and present — in science, math, engineering, and technology. The event has been held every October since the year 2009.

POETICAL SCIENCE

Lovelace called herself a "poetical scientist." Her ideas were not always practical. She tried, but failed, to create:

★ A steam-powered flying machine.

★ A surefire scheme to win at gambling.

★ A mathematical explanation for the way in which the brain produces thoughts.

"My **scientific studies** have afforded
me **great gratification**."

GREGOR MENDEL

I was really brainy and especially good at physics and math. Although I came from a poor farming family, my parents managed to put me through college. Then I surprised everyone by becoming a monk — no one saw that coming! Thankfully, the order I joined had facilities for scientific experiments and sent me to study in Vienna.

Hybrids and Their Genes

I knew about growing plants and decided to study how they inherited their different characteristics. Everyone knew you could create a hybrid by crossbreeding one plant with another, but how this worked remained a scientific mystery.

For eight years, I grew peas in the monastery garden and followed them from generation to generation. I cross-fertilized them and recorded the results —for instance, what happened if a green-seeded pea was crossed with a yellow-seeded pea. Using my knowledge of math to analyze the results statistically, I developed rules governing inheritance and identified what were later called "genes." But no one could grasp what I'd achieved. I lived the rest of my monastic life without acknowledgment, my science all but forgotten.

TIME LINE

1822 Born in Moravia, then part of the Austrian Empire, now in the Czech Republic

1854 Begins experiments with pea plants at Augustinian monastery in Brno, Moravia

1866 Publishes his research paper *Experiments on Plant Hybridization*

1868 Becomes abbot of the monastery

1884 Dies in Brno, Moravia

MENDELIAN HEREDITY

Mendel's experiments showed that a tall plant crossed with a short plant made a hybrid that was tall or short, but never medium-sized. He deduced that the hybrid inherited two versions of the gene for each trait — one from each parent — and that the offspring would always resemble one parent or the other.

LEGACY

Austrian scientist Gregor Mendel laid the basis for modern genetics. His brilliant research established many of the accepted principles by which heredity works — that is, how certain characteristics pass from one generation to the next.

PESKY BEES

As well as experimenting with peas, Mendel studied bees, which he bred in special hives. Unfortunately, his bees had a nasty habit of stinging the other monks at the monastery. After several complaints, Mendel was forced to get rid of his fuzzy friends.

DOMINANT GENES

Mendel established that some genes were **dominant** (stronger) and others **recessive** (weaker). If a pure purple-flowered plant crossed with a pure white-flowered plant produced offspring with purple flowers, that meant the gene for purple was dominant.

?
Why was Mendel's work ignored?

People failed to look carefully at Mendel's work, because no one expected groundbreaking science to come from an Austrian monk. Around 1900, when other scientists started finding the same results, they were forced to admit that Mendel had gotten there first.

"A man who dares to **waste one hour** of time
has not discovered **the value of life.**"

CHARLES DARWIN

An amateur naturalist, at the age of twenty-two, I jumped at the chance to sail as a passenger on a Royal Navy ship, HMS *Beagle*, which was surveying the uncharted coasts of South America. We really got around on the five-year voyage, and I observed thousands of strange animals and plants from the most exotic locations, including the Brazilian rain forest and the Galápagos Islands.

Evolutionary Thinking

Once back in England, I wrote the story of my travels and the wonders I had seen, and became a minor celebrity. I settled into a quiet domestic life, but never stopped investigating nature. I spent years at home, making painstaking studies of barnacles and earthworms and insect-eating plants.

Mulling over my time on the *Beagle*, I figured out a theory to explain life on Earth. When I published my ideas on evolution through natural selection, the newspapers caricatured me as a monkey, because I said humans were descended from apes. Despite resistance from some religious groups, however, my views were accepted by scientists as a breakthrough in the understanding of humans and nature.

TIME LINE

1809 Born in Shropshire, England

1831–1836 Sails around the world on board HMS *Beagle*

1859 Writes his book *On the Origin of Species*

1871 Publishes *The Descent of Man* discussing his theories on the origins of human beings

1882 Dies in Kent, England

LEGACY

English naturalist Charles Darwin is famous for his theory that all new species evolve through natural selection, and that humans also developed in this way. Darwin's theory of evolution forms the basis for modern life sciences.

GREAT MINDS

French naturalist **Jean-Baptiste Lamarck** (1744–1829) produced the first theory of evolution in 1802. But he claimed animals progressed through effort — that giraffes lengthened their necks by stretching for high leaves and then passed the longer neck on to their offspring. Darwin proved that this was completely wrong.

GALÁPAGOS BREAKTHROUGH

On board HMS *Beagle*, Darwin visited the Galápagos Islands in the Pacific in 1835. He found that some closely related birds existed as different species on different islands. He concluded that they had evolved from the same original species.

?

Did the Church reject Darwin's theory?
Some Christians attacked Darwin's theory, because it contradicted the Bible story of the creation and because it said humans were descended from apes. But the Church of England accepted Darwin's science, and he was buried in Westminster Abbey.

TOP BREEDERS

Darwin noticed that farmers developed beefier cows or fatter hogs by selecting certain animals for breeding. He suggested that evolution worked in the same way, and that the struggle for survival ensured that those animals best adapted to their environment would breed. He called this "natural selection."

"Science knows no country, because knowledge belongs to humanity."

LOUIS PASTEUR

Human history was riddled with killer diseases that struck for no apparent reason. Humans had little defense against them and no one knew what to do about it . . . until I came along, that is.

Seeing Small

Hats off to the microscope, which showed me a world of tiny microorganisms that were invisible to the naked eye. I discovered they were the key to many things that had never been properly understood — why old milk turned sour, for example. Most important of all, I learned that ultrasmall germs caused diseases and infected wounds. OK, so I wasn't the first person to think this, but I did prove it!

At the time, rabies was a much-feared, often fatal disease, caught from infected dogs. As luck would have it, I developed a vaccine just as nine-year-old Joseph Meister was badly bitten by a rabid dog. I tested my vaccine on the boy and the disease failed to develop — the vaccine had worked! Even today, anyone at risk from the disease, be they man or beast, is vaccinated against it. Well, I became a national hero and set up an institute to carry on my good work after my death.

TIME LINE

1822 Born in Dole, France

1862 Experiments with "pasteurization" of wine and beer

1885 Tests the first rabies vaccine

1888 Founds the Pasteur Institute

1895 Dies in Paris, France

GREAT MINDS

British surgeon **Joseph Lister** (1827–1912) applied Pasteur's ideas on infection to surgical procedures. By sterilizing his surgical instruments and cleaning wounds carefully when operating, Lister saved the lives of thousands of patients who would otherwise have died of infections.

MAGGOTS AND GERMS

Some scientists believed in "spontaneous generation" — that dead meat produced maggots and that dirt made germs. In 1862, Louis Pasteur proved by experiment that no life appeared in sterilized dead matter if it was sealed from its surroundings. Only flies made maggots and only germs made germs.

LEGACY

Louis Pasteur was a French microbiologist who proved that diseases were spread by infection with germs. As well as developing vaccines to counter killer diseases, he revolutionized food safety with his technique of "pasteurization."

PERSONAL MOTIVATION

Pasteur and his wife had five children. Two of them died of typhoid, an infectious disease for which there was no cure at the time. This family tragedy is said to have motivated Pasteur in his search for ways of preventing or curing such diseases.

?

What is pasteurization?
Pasteurization is a technique used in food processing. It involves heating a food or drink to a high enough temperature to kill microorganisms and then cooling it down again. The process prolongs the shelf life of the food or drink, and stops it from being a danger to human health.

THE MODERN ERA

The modern era saw an explosion — literally, in some cases — of all things scientific. The world watched agog as our heroes of science proved that the unimaginable could, in fact, become reality. World firsts included the first antibiotic, the first nuclear explosion, and the first Nobel Prize. Great breakthroughs saw the discovery of the structure of DNA and that the universe is expanding. But this modern era is not over. The milestones of this last century are, like those of the centuries before them, simply the start of a new scientific age.

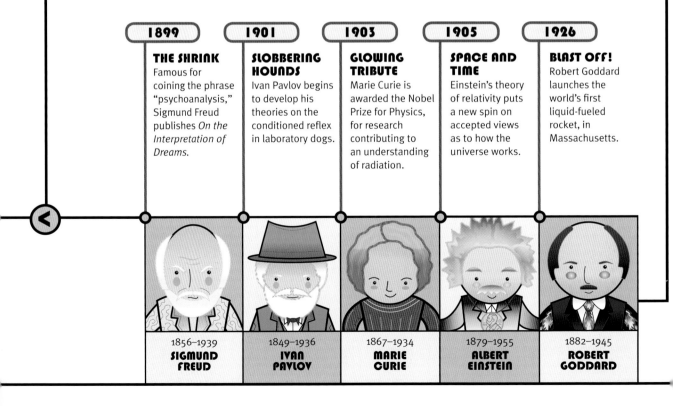

1899
THE SHRINK
Famous for coining the phrase "psychoanalysis," Sigmund Freud publishes *On the Interpretation of Dreams*.

1901
SLOBBERING HOUNDS
Ivan Pavlov begins to develop his theories on the conditioned reflex in laboratory dogs.

1903
GLOWING TRIBUTE
Marie Curie is awarded the Nobel Prize for Physics, for research contributing to an understanding of radiation.

1905
SPACE AND TIME
Einstein's theory of relativity puts a new spin on accepted views as to how the universe works.

1926
BLAST OFF!
Robert Goddard launches the world's first liquid-fueled rocket, in Massachusetts.

1856–1939
SIGMUND FREUD

1849–1936
IVAN PAVLOV

1867–1934
MARIE CURIE

1879–1955
ALBERT EINSTEIN

1882–1945
ROBERT GODDARD

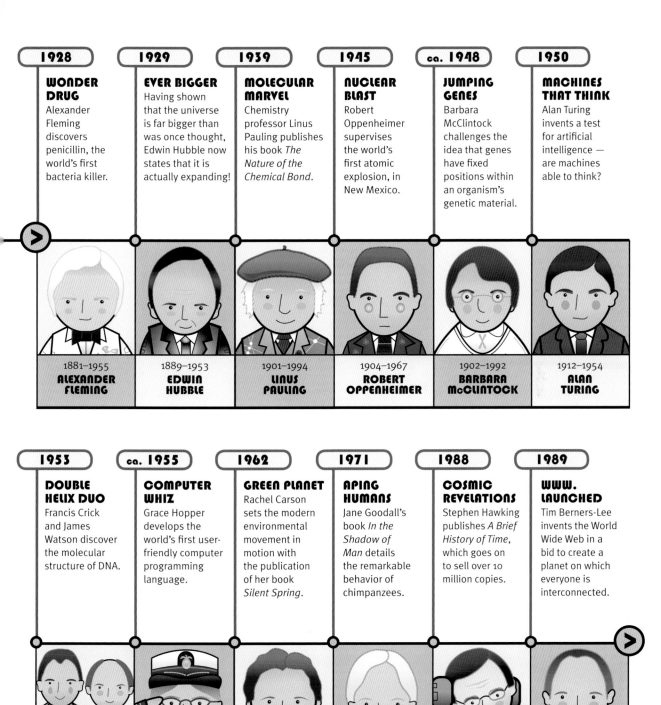

1928
WONDER DRUG
Alexander Fleming discovers penicillin, the world's first bacteria killer.

1929
EVER BIGGER
Having shown that the universe is far bigger than was once thought, Edwin Hubble now states that it is actually expanding!

1939
MOLECULAR MARVEL
Chemistry professor Linus Pauling publishes his book *The Nature of the Chemical Bond*.

1945
NUCLEAR BLAST
Robert Oppenheimer supervises the world's first atomic explosion, in New Mexico.

ca. 1948
JUMPING GENES
Barbara McClintock challenges the idea that genes have fixed positions within an organism's genetic material.

1950
MACHINES THAT THINK
Alan Turing invents a test for artificial intelligence — are machines able to think?

1881–1955
ALEXANDER FLEMING

1889–1953
EDWIN HUBBLE

1901–1994
LINUS PAULING

1904–1967
ROBERT OPPENHEIMER

1902–1992
BARBARA McCLINTOCK

1912–1954
ALAN TURING

1953
DOUBLE HELIX DUO
Francis Crick and James Watson discover the molecular structure of DNA.

ca. 1955
COMPUTER WHIZ
Grace Hopper develops the world's first user-friendly computer programming language.

1962
GREEN PLANET
Rachel Carson sets the modern environmental movement in motion with the publication of her book *Silent Spring*.

1971
APING HUMANS
Jane Goodall's book *In the Shadow of Man* details the remarkable behavior of chimpanzees.

1988
COSMIC REVELATIONS
Stephen Hawking publishes *A Brief History of Time*, which goes on to sell over 10 million copies.

1989
WWW. LAUNCHED
Tim Berners-Lee invents the World Wide Web in a bid to create a planet on which everyone is interconnected.

1916–2004/b. 1928
CRICK & WATSON

1906–1992
GRACE HOPPER

1907–1964
RACHEL CARSON

b. 1934
JANE GOODALL

b. 1942
STEPHEN HAWKING

b. 1955
TIM BERNERS-LEE

"Being entirely **honest** with oneself is a **good exercise.**"

SIGMUND FREUD

Having gone to medical school, I was quick to see that some patients were sick in ways that could not be seen. Folks were troubled by weird anxieties. Some of my cases were really odd, and I gave them funny names like "Rat Man" and "Wolf Man."

The World's Most Famous Shrink

Gradually, I developed a theory. People were driven by primitive urges and emotions, I said. These urges were unconscious and, often, the opposite of what people believed they felt. I made it my job to uncover these hidden feelings by talking to my patients, using a process I called psychoanalysis. I hoped that if they faced their true selves, they'd be cured. I had ideas about all aspects of human behavior — in relationships, in religion, in childhood, and even in death. Some of my ideas seemed bizarre and I offended a lot of people. Still, I became ultra-famous and my ideas changed the way people thought about the world.

I'd always lived in Austria. Then, in 1938, the Nazis took over the country. They hated me because I was Jewish and they hated Jews. I had to flee and died in exile in London soon after.

TIME LINE

1856 Born in Freiberg, Austria

1899 Publishes *The Interpretation of Dreams*

1910 Founds the International Psychoanalytic Association

1938 Flees to London, England, to escape the Nazis

1939 Dies in London, England

LEGACY

Doctor Sigmund Freud set out to understand the human mind and to explain emotional conflicts and irrational behavior. His theories led him to invent psychoanalysis as a talking cure for disorders of the mind, such as anxiety and depression.

FREUDIAN SLIP

Freud claimed that unconscious feelings sometimes reveal themselves in accidental mistakes, especially slips of the tongue. So somebody who, in reality, dislikes the supposed friend he or she is meeting might say: "I'm mad to see you," instead of "I'm glad to see you."

GREAT MINDS

Swiss psychologist **Carl Jung** (1875–1961) was a follower of Freud but broke away to develop his own ideas. He grouped people as outgoing extroverts and quieter introverts, terms we still use today. He also had out-of-the-box ideas like the "collective unconscious," which claimed every human mind possessed information common to all people, based on experiences from generations long gone.

?

Was Freud a true scientist?
Freud certainly meant to be a scientist — to discover hard facts that proved his theories — and hoped future study of the brain would achieve this. But many critics think psychoanalysis is just a smart-sounding theory that no one can actually prove.

ALL IN THE MIND

Freud's key ideas include the following:

★ Our rational self, the ego, doesn't control our behavior. Instead, it is driven by unconscious impulses.

★ Dreams reveal people's secret desires, if interpreted correctly.

★ Psychoanalysis can cure mental problems. By talking with patients, they are able to come to terms with their unconscious wishes.

"The **nervous system** is the most **complex** and **delicate** instrument on our planet."

IVAN PAVLOV

The son of a priest, I tried following in my dad's footsteps but revolted and ran off to study in St. Petersburg. I was fascinated by physiology, the study of how the body works. I got my own lab at the Institute of Experimental Medicine, where I spent years observing the digestive system of dogs. Not much glamour there, you might say, but it won me a Nobel Prize!

Hungry Hounds

My genius lay in spit! One aspect of digestion is salivation. My lab dogs drooled big-time whenever they saw food. This reflex was completely natural — find a picture of something tasty, and you'll salivate, too. One day, I saw the hounds slobbering even though their feed-time assistant was empty-handed. I figured out that it was possible to teach the dogs to salivate when a buzzer sounded, by associating the ringing with food. I called this a conditioned reflex.

But these were turbulent times. In 1917, there was a revolution. A new government turned the Russian Empire into the communist Soviet Union. I loathed the communists, but they left me to my work. When I died I was given a hero's funeral.

TIME LINE

1849 Born in Ryazan, Russia

1891 Founds a physiology lab at the Institute of Experimental Medicine in St. Petersburg

1901 Begins work on conditioned reflexes in dogs

1904 Awarded Nobel Prize

1936 Dies in St. Petersburg (then Leningrad), Russia

TAKING THE CURE

Pavlov's conditioning has been used to cure people addicted to alcohol. If something that induces a feeling of nausea is added to an alcoholic drink, it is not long before the drinker associates the nausea with the drink. He or she then starts to feel ill, even at the sight of alcohol, so ends the harmful addiction.

LEGACY

Russian scientist Ivan Pavlov is best known for the experiments he carried out on his laboratory dogs. His work allowed him to explore the nervous system and led to an important breakthrough in the study of human psychology.

GREAT MINDS

American psychologist **John B. Watson** (1878–1958) applied Pavlov's conditioning to humans. In one experiment, he made a frightening noise with a hammer each time a child, "little Albert," touched a pet rat. The boy quickly developed a fear of rats. Watson founded the behaviorist school of psychology.

?

Were Pavlov's experiments cruel to animals?
Pavlov was a dog lover, but there is no doubt his lab animals suffered. He experimented on his dogs ruthlessly, operating on them more than once and even starving them. No researcher would be allowed to treat dogs in that way today.

STRANGE BUT TRUE!

Pavlov's dogs produced large quantities of stomach juices during his experiments with them. His laboratory bottled these juices and sold them to doctors and pharmacies as a popular medicine for treating human stomach ailments.

"All that **I saw** and **learned** . . . was like a **new world** opened to me, the world of **science** . . ."

MARIE CURIE

Ra **Po**

My career was a triumph, not just for science but for women, too. When I was young, girls were told that science was for boys. What was that all about, you might ask. I sure wasn't listening!

I left my homeland, Poland, and went to study in Paris, France. I was so short on money, I almost starved. Then I had a lucky break. I met and married a Frenchman, Pierre Curie, who shared my passion for science. Together, we set about trying to find the source of what the two of us called "radioactivity," a strange radiation that gave our hands a luminous glow in the dark. We had very few resources but, eventually we found tiny amounts of two radioactive elements no one had ever seen before. We called them polonium and radium.

Nobel Victory

Pierre died in 1906, but I continued with our work. The first female professor at the University of Paris, I won renown across the globe — and the glory of being the only woman ever to win two Nobel Prizes! I always hoped the radiation from radium would cure many diseases, but I failed to notice the harm it was causing me, resulting in my death.

TIME LINE

1867 Born in Warsaw, Poland, as Marie Sklodowska

1895 Marries Pierre Curie in Paris

1898 Discovers radium and polonium

1903 Wins Nobel Prize in Physics

1911 Wins Nobel Prize in Chemistry

1934 Dies in France

LEGACY

Marie Curie discovered radium, a chemical element that produces radiation. It had gone unnoticed before because it existed in tiny amounts hidden in other minerals. Curie's death from bone cancer highlighted the dangers of exposure to radiation.

GREAT MINDS

In 1895 German scientist **Wilhelm Röntgen** (1845–1923) discovered a type of invisible radiation he called X rays. He realized they could be used to see inside the body and produced skeletal images of his wife's hand. He was awarded the first-ever Nobel Prize in Physics (1901).

A WOMAN'S LOT

Marie Curie had to fight prejudice because of her gender. As a young woman in Poland, she couldn't go to university because they were for men only. In France, she was never elected to the Academy of Sciences, which did not admit its first female member until 1962.

? Didn't Curie know radiation was harmful?

Today we know that radiation can cause cancers and other serious damage to the body. Anyone handling radium wears protective clothing. But, unfortunately, Marie Curie had no idea radioactive radium was harmful. She even used to carry it around in her pockets.

CURIE AT WAR

When France went to war with Germany in 1914, Marie Curie set up the first mobile X-ray units to help treat wounded soldiers. The grateful troops called her small X-ray trucks **Little Curies** in her honor. At the time, Curie also introduced the use of radon, a radioactive gas produced by radium, to sterilize soldiers' wounds.

"Why is it that **nobody understands me** and **everybody likes me?**"

$E=mc^2$

ALBERT EINSTEIN

With crazy hair and (some might say) harebrained ideas, I just screamed mad professor. I had a regular office job but, really, I was a genius physicist. "Relativity" was my thing: I realized that nothing in the universe was fixed. Even space could warp and time could stretch or shrink. It simply depended on your point of view.

When I published my theory of relativity, only physicists took notice. Then, in 1919, astronomers observing an eclipse of the sun saw light bent by gravity, just as I had predicted. That told them!

A Troubled Mind

In 1933, the Nazis came to power in Germany and began persecuting Jews. Being Jewish, I fled to America.

Inspired by my equation $E = mc^2$, scientists tried to make an atom bomb. I warned the US president that the Nazis might get there first and this triggered America's program. I didn't feel good about my role in the creation of the atom bomb, and I later campaigned for a world government to end all wars. Ever the scientist, all I really wanted was a unified theory of everything — one single explanation for all the forces in the universe. I never found it!

TIME LINE

1879 Born in Ulm, Germany

1905 Publishes the special theory of relativity

1921 Wins the Nobel Prize in Physics

1933 Leaves Germany for the United States

1939 Warns that Germany is building a nuclear bomb

1955 Dies in Princeton, New Jersey

GREAT MINDS

Scottish physicist **James Clerk Maxwell** (1831–1879) prepared the way for Einstein's relativity by linking electricity, magnetism, and light in a single theory of electromagnetic fields. Between them, Maxwell and Einstein made Isaac Newton's simpler view of the universe outdated.

CURIOUS DISCOVERIES

Einstein showed that:

★ A person ages more slowly the faster he or she travels. He claimed astronauts return from space younger than if they'd stayed on Earth.

★ The faster an object travels, the smaller it becomes.

★ Gravity bends light, an effect that creates "black holes" in space.

LEGACY

With his theory of relativity, Albert Einstein fundamentally changed our understanding of the universe, transforming how we think about the nature of space and time. His work paved the way for the development of atomic energy.

MIGHTY EQUATION

Einstein said that atoms (tiny particles) of matter contain a huge amount of energy. His equation $E = mc^2$ means that energy (E) is equal to mass (m) times the speed of light (c) squared. Unlocking the energy in the atom created a bomb that could destroy whole cities.

?

So what exactly is relativity?
Einstein describes relativity using a passenger on a moving train who drops a rock out of the window. The passenger sees the rock fall straight down. Someone watching alongside the track, however, sees the rock follow a curved path as it falls. Both are right from their own point of view.

"The **dream** of yesterday is the **hope** of today and the **reality** of tomorrow."

ROBERT GODDARD

As a kid I was thrilled by science fiction stories of aliens visiting Earth and journeys to the moon. At the time, serious scientists thought these were just fantasies, yet I had an idea in my head and it just wouldn't go away.

Rocket Science

I studied physics and figured out that it really was possible to fire a rocket to the edge of Earth's atmosphere and beyond — say, even to the moon. But my ideas were ridiculed and I decided to keep my work to myself. Worse still, financial backing for rocket experiments was hard to find and progress was slow. I developed rockets fueled by liquid oxygen and gasoline. I successfully tested my first rocket at a farm in Massachusetts in 1926.

Later on, I made more than thirty test launches in the New Mexico desert. My rockets climbed nine thousand feet — high enough to test guidance and control systems. Success at last, you might think! But when the United States entered World War II in 1941, could I interest the military in my rockets? No sir! By the time I died, it was the Germans who'd made rocket missiles a reality.

TIME LINE

1882 Born in Worcester, Massachusetts

1919 States his theory of rocket space flight

1926 Launches first liquid-fueled rocket

1930 Begins experiments at Roswell, New Mexico

1945 Dies in Baltimore, Maryland

LEGACY

American physicist Robert Goddard prepared the way for the great age of space exploration. His practical experiments involving rockets, and calculations of how space flight would work, proved that it was possible to travel to the moon.

GREAT MINDS

Wernher von Braun (1912–1977) designed the German V-2 rocket, the world's first long-range missile. It entered service in 1944. After World War II, von Braun moved to the United States and became a key figure in developing rockets for the American space program.

HUMBLE APOLOGY

In 1920, the **New York Times** ridiculed Goddard for suggesting that a rocket could work in the vacuum of space. It wasn't until forty-nine years later, when the *Apollo 11* mission took off to land a human on the moon, that the newspaper printed a correction apologizing for its error.

?

Was Goddard too secretive?
Goddard was reluctant to share the results of his rocket experiments. Arguably, this held up the development of rockets in the United States, but Goddard had trouble convincing the US military that his rockets could be of interest to them in the first place!

DAWN OF A NEW SPACE AGE

Goddard's space-related inventions include:

★ The first liquid-fueled rocket engine.

★ A guidance system using moveable vanes (fins) attached to the rocket.

★ A gyroscopic control system to stabilize the rocket in flight.

"One sometimes **finds** what one is **not looking for** . . ."

ALEXANDER FLEMING

Working as a professor at a hospital medical school in London, it was my job to study the bacteria that caused deadly infections. In 1928, I returned from summer vacation to find mold growing on samples of bacteria I'd left lying around the lab. (I'll be honest, I was no neat freak!) Looking closely, I noticed something strange: The mold had killed the bacteria . . .

A Miracle Cure?

Quite by chance, I'd found a natural antibiotic: penicillin. I knew how important this discovery could be, because I'd been a doctor during World War I, when thousands of soldiers had died of infected wounds. We doctors knew bacteria caused the infections, but our antiseptics were powerless against them. I strived but failed to turn my mold into a usable drug.

In 1939, World War II broke out and the search for effective antibiotics became urgent. Researchers in Oxford, England, found a way to make pure penicillin and governments funded mass production of the drug. By the war's end, it was being used to treat wounded US and British soldiers, and my pioneering efforts made me famous.

TIME LINE

1881 Born in Ayrshire, Scotland

1914–1918 Serves in the Royal Medical Corps during World War I

1928 Discovers penicillin while studying influenza

1945 Shares the Nobel Prize in Medicine

1955 Dies in London, England

PURE LUCK

The discovery of penicillin is an example of serendipity — the happy chance when a researcher stumbles upon something he or she wasn't actually looking for in the first place. Another example of this is the **microwave oven**, which was conceived in 1945 when a radar engineer, Percy Spencer, noticed the energy waves from the radar had melted his candy bar.

LEGACY

Scottish medical scientist Alexander Fleming discovered the world's first bacteria killer. Developed into a practical drug by others, penicillin gave doctors their first effective weapon in fighting infection and saved millions of lives.

NOSE JOB

As well as penicillin, Fleming discovered **lysozyme**, which also counters infection. He found it in the nose mucus (that's "snot" to you) of a patient with a cold. When the patient's nose dripped into a dish of bacteria, it made the bacteria disintegrate.

PENICILLIN PIONEERS

Working in Oxford, England, Australian researcher **Howard Florey** (1898–1968) and German-born British scientist **Ernst Chain** (1906–1979) made the first penicillin suitable for medical use in 1941. They were awarded the Nobel Prize jointly with Fleming in 1945.

?

Was Fleming just lucky?
Fleming was lucky, but he was smart, too. He saw the significance of the mold's effect on his bacteria, which any other person may well have missed. And for years he kept on trying to develop penicillin as a drug, until others completed the work.

"Man **explores** the universe around him
and calls the adventure **science.**"

EDWIN HUBBLE

I came late to astronomy, but once I'd arrived, there was no turning back. Working at the Mount Wilson Observatory in Pasadena, California, I studied the potential of Hooker, the newest, most powerful telescope in the world. Astronomers had used it to estimate the size of our galaxy, the Milky Way. They said it was three hundred thousand light-years across. Well, if one light-year is close to six trillion miles (9.5 trillion km), that's pretty big, no?

I was thinking bigger! My own observations using Hooker showed that the fuzzy clusters of stars we call nebulae are far beyond the Milky Way — way out in deep space — and that our galaxy is just one of many. People were stunned at the sheer size of the universe I had uncovered.

The Expanding Universe
Then I made another amazing observation. All other galaxies are speeding away from ours and away from one another — the universe is expanding! This discovery gave scientists a problem to chew on for decades. As for me, I went on stargazing for the rest of my life and died just as they were about to award me the Nobel Prize.

TIME LINE

1889 Born in Marshfield, Missouri

1919 Begins lifelong work at Mount Wilson Observatory, California

1925 Announces discovery of galaxies beyond the Milky Way

1929 States that the universe is expanding

1953 Dies in San Marino, California

LEGACY
Edwin Hubble counts as one of the great modern astronomers. Not only did he show that the universe was far larger than anyone had previously imagined, but he was the first to suggest that it was actually expanding.

GREAT MINDS
Hubble worked alongside **Milton Humason** (1891–1972), a high school dropout who had once delivered equipment to the observatory by mule. Taken on as janitor, he got to use the telescope and turned out to be a good observer. He became known as an astronomer in his own right — without a single degree or diploma.

EXPANSION THEORY
Hubble observed that the farther away a galaxy is in space, the faster it is moving away from Earth. This is called **Hubble's Law**. It is a prime piece of evidence that shows that the whole universe must, indeed, be expanding.

?
How did Hubble know space was expanding?
The light coming from an object is different if the object is moving toward you or going away — just as a car horn sounds different whether approaching or receding. By analyzing the light from stars, Hubble could tell the majority were traveling ever farther away.

BEYOND THE MILKY WAY
The spectacular space telescope launched into Earth's orbit by NASA in 1990 is named after Edwin Hubble. Clear of Earth's atmosphere, the **Hubble Space Telescope** has the ability to look far into deep space and record amazing images of the distant galaxies it spies.

"Chemistry is **wonderful!**"

LINUS PAULING

Chemistry gave me such a buzz, I felt sorry for those who knew nothing about it. I loved it so much that I set up a lab in the basement of our home when I was a kid. It's no surprise that I studied science in college and became a professor at Caltech.

Career Highs and Lows

I researched the structure of molecules and what holds them together. You may not find that exciting, but I did — others did, too. When I published my book *The Nature of the Chemical Bond,* I became a superstar (in the science world, at least).

During World War II, I contributed to the US war effort but later worried about nuclear weapons. Objecting to atom bomb tests, I produced scientific evidence for the harmful effects of nuclear fallout. Some saw my activities as "un-American" and I had my passport taken away. Later, nuclear tests in the atmosphere were stopped.

Turning my attention to public health, I promoted good old vitamin C as a wonder cure for everything from colds to cancer. Sure, not everyone agreed with all I said, but no one doubted I was a great scientist.

TIME LINE

1901 Born in Portland, Oregon

1927 Becomes a professor at California Institute of Technology

1939 Publishes key book *The Nature of the Chemical Bond*

1954 Awarded Nobel Prize in Chemistry

1958 Publishes antiwar book *No More War!*

1962 Awarded Nobel Peace Prize

1994 Dies in Big Sur, California

FAST FACTS

Pauling was:

✴ The scientist who related the latest discoveries of physics to the study of chemistry.

✴ One of the founding fathers of molecular biology — the study of life at the level of molecules.

✴ A pioneer of environmental health studies.

MOLECULAR MEDICINE

In 1949 Pauling showed that **sickle-cell disease**, an inherited blood disorder, was caused by an abnormality in molecules in red blood cells. It was the first time a disease had been traced to the molecular level. The event opened up a whole new field of medical science.

LEGACY

Pauling was one of the most influential scientists of the twentieth century. His work in molecular chemistry led to important medical advances. A noted peace campaigner, he is the only person to have won two unshared Nobel Prizes.

NUCLEAR INFLUENCE

Linus Pauling's wife, **Ava Helen Pauling** (1903–1981), was a peace activist and antinuclear campaigner. She triggered her husband's concern about nuclear tests and perhaps should have shared his Nobel Peace Prize in 1962.

?

Did Pauling stop nuclear tests?
In the 1950s, nuclear bombs were tested in deserts and on islands. Pauling showed that the nuclear fallout was causing birth defects and cancers. Partly because of Pauling's work, in 1963, an international agreement was signed banning nuclear tests aboveground.

"The peoples of this world **must unite** or they **will perish.**"

ROBERT OPPENHEIMER

I was famous as the man who made the atom bomb — something I had mixed feelings about. In the 1930s, I'd been one of several physicists guessing how big a bang we'd get if we split the atom. In 1942, with the United States at war, I was asked to head a group of scientists in the top-secret Manhattan Project. Our mission? To make the most powerful bomb ever. Explosive stuff!

Building the Bomb
An oddball bunch of international scientists, we assembled at Los Alamos, New Mexico. My role was to coordinate our efforts. When I witnessed the first awesome nuclear explosion in 1945, I was delighted we had succeeded but troubled by what such power might mean for the world.

After the war, my efforts to establish international control over nuclear power through the United Nations fell on deaf ears. Instead, I was branded anti-American and even suspected of spying for the Soviet Union! It was nonsense, of course, but it hurt! Thankfully, my reputation was restored when I was granted a lifetime achievement award by President John F. Kennedy.

TIME LINE

1904 Born in New York City

1929 Works in California at Berkeley and Caltech

1942 Takes a leading role in the Manhattan Project

1945 Supervises the first atomic explosion

1953 Declared a security risk

1967 Dies in Princeton, New Jersey

LEGACY
Nuclear physicist Robert Oppenheimer was the scientific head of the Manhattan Project, which produced the world's first atom bombs. He excelled as a coordinator of the work of other scientists and as a scientific adviser to the government.

GREAT MINDS
Italian **Enrico Fermi** (1901–1954) was a nuclear physicist who had immigrated to the United States. He worked with Oppenheimer on the atom bomb project. In 1942, he built the world's first nuclear reactor in Chicago and used it to achieve the first nuclear chain reaction.

NOBEL NONSENSE
Austrian physicist **Lise Meitner** (1878–1968) played a key role in identifying the splitting of the atom in uranium in 1939. Her male colleague **Otto Hahn** was awarded a Nobel Prize but Meitner was not, an example of blatant sexism in science.

?
How did the atom bomb work?
Scientists knew that splitting an atom of matter would release energy. The key to the bomb was setting up a chain reaction in which each atom split would release particles, causing other atoms to split. The total effect was then huge.

FIRST EXPLOSIONS
Oppenheimer and his colleagues staged the first nuclear test in the desert at Los Alamos on July 16, 1945. The explosion was equal to twenty thousand tons of TNT and made a mushroom cloud 7.5 miles (12 km) high. Atom bombs were used as weapons in the war and were dropped on two Japanese cities the following month.

"When you **know** you're right,
you **don't care** what others think."

McCLINTOCK

A loner through and through, nothing pleased me more than studying science. Mom was horrified. She said no man would marry me if I became a scientist. As if I cared! At least Dad gave me his backing, so I got to study botany at Cornell.

Jumping Genes

I developed an interest in a completely new field of science, studying the genome in plant cells — that's the part containing the cell's genetic material. Corn proved ideal for this research, and I studied the plant for most of my adult life. Winning recognition as a leading scientist had been a cakewalk, but when I started talking about "jumping genes," other scientists thought I'd lost it. I just knew that genes could change position within a genome, while everyone else insisted they were fixed.

Eventually, other scientists caught up with me and they had to admit I'd gotten there first. They even awarded me a Nobel Prize . . . thirty years after my most important work had been done. I didn't mind the wait. My research had given me so much pleasure over the years, I didn't need any other reward. And I never did marry, as it happened!

TIME LINE

1902 Born in Hartford, Connecticut

1931 Publishes first genetic map for corn

1944 Elected to the National Academy of Sciences

1983 Awarded the Nobel Prize for Physiology or Medicine

1992 Dies in Huntington, New York

GENE DEVELOPMENT

McClintock's work was groundbreaking:

★ She showed that particular genes were linked to specific traits in plants.

★ She discovered that some genes can change position in a chromosome (jumping genes).

★ She traced the genetic evolution of corn varieties.

LEGACY

Barbara McClintock was the first geneticist to suggest that an organism's genome is changeable rather than fixed. Later, her ideas became invaluable to scientists seeking to understand the complex nature of genes and how they function.

VEGGIE FRIENDS

McClintock combined her passion for science with a love of plants. She was impressed by how sensitive plants were in many ways and said she was never comfortable walking on grass. She empathized with the corn plants she studied, claiming that she knew each one individually.

GIRL POWER

✳ **Florence Sabin** (1871–1953), a medical scientist, was the first woman elected a full member of the National Academy of Sciences, in 1925.

✳ Biochemist **Gerti Cori** (1896–1957) became the first American woman scientist to win a Nobel Prize, in 1947.

?

Why did McClintock's work go largely ignored?
Some people think that resistance to McClintock's theory of jumping genes came from male scientists who wouldn't listen seriously to a female colleague. But, really, it was more that her ideas were just too unexpected for them to believe.

"I am **building a brain.**"

ALAN TURING

Educated at a pricey private school, then at Cambridge University, I had the upbringing of a typical English gentleman. But "typical" ended there. As a young man, I had an idea for a universal machine that would be able to calculate any sum and solve all logical problems. Sound like a computer? It was mind-blowing in my day.

Cracking Codes

During World War II, a group of brilliant oddballs like me were assembled at Bletchley Park in England to crack German secret codes. Sure, I had the right mind for this work, but I knew a machine would be better. I created the super-speedy Bombe, which helped decode German Enigma messages. Groundbreaking, yes, but did it make me famous? No! It was all hush-hush, of course!

After the war I helped develop early computers. The idea of artificial intelligence fascinated me. Could a machine really think? I was investigating this and other amazing questions when I was arrested for being gay, which was a crime at the time. I never recovered from the experience and died of cyanide poisoning.

TIME LINE

1912 Born in London, England

1936 Proposes idea of universal computing machine

1939–1945 Works as Enigma code breaker

1950 Invents "Turing test" for artificial intelligence

1951 Elected a fellow of the Royal Society

1954 Dies in Cheshire, England

LEGACY

British mathematician Alan Turing was a pioneer of computer science. He did invaluable work as a code breaker during World War II, built early computers, and invented a test to determine whether a machine could think intelligently.

TURING TEST

In order to test whether a machine could think, Turing suggested an imitation game, in which a scientist communicates separately with a human in one room and a computer in another. If the computer imitates the human so successfully that the scientist can't tell which is which, it has proved itself intelligent.

SECRET SOCIETY

The brainy folks who worked at Britain's top-secret **Bletchley Park** decoding center during World War II included people good at math, puzzles, and chess, as well as computer geeks like Turing. Bletchley Park was kept a secret until thirty years after the war's end.

? What was Enigma?

During World War II, German forces used the Enigma machine to put messages into code. By adjusting its rotors and cables, an operator could encode messages in billions of different ways. The Germans considered the Enigma code unbreakable, but Turing cracked it.

COMPUTER WHIZ

Turing is renowned for:

* Producing the first precise description of a modern computer and how it would work.
* Cracking the German Navy's Enigma code messages during World War II.
* Investigating the possibility of artificial intelligence.

"We had **found** the **secret** of life."

WATSON AND CRICK

I'm Francis Crick, one half of the double-helix duo. I met the other half, James Watson, while we were both working at the Cavendish Laboratory in Cambridge, England, in 1951. Watson was an amazingly bright kid who'd attended the University of Chicago at age 15. I was much older than he was, but we just hit it off.

Watson's Challenge

Watson's dream was to pin down the molecular structure of DNA (deoxyribonucleic acid) — the stuff that makes up our genes. Scientists in American labs were close to working it out, and Watson wanted to beat them to it. I joined the young gun in his quest. And we cracked it, too! We identified DNA as a double helix — two entwined strands that were capable of separating and copying themselves. Other scientists took some convincing, and it was years before our discovery was acknowledged with a Nobel Prize.

In the meantime, Watson and I went our separate ways. Watson helped get the Human Genome Project up and running, while I turned to studying the brain and consciousness at the Salk Institute, California.

TIME LINE

1916 Francis Crick born in Northampton, England

1928 James Watson born in Chicago, Illinois

1953 Jointly discover the molecular structure of DNA

1962 Jointly awarded Nobel Prize

1968 Watson publishes book *The Double Helix*

2004 Francis Crick dies in San Diego, California

DNA DISCOVERIES

Among their achievements, Watson and Crick:

★ Found that the structure of a DNA molecule is a double helix.

★ Established how genetic information is chemically encoded in DNA.

★ Discovered how DNA makes copies of itself, whereby the double helix splits and each half forms a new pair.

LEGACY

Together, Watson and Crick discovered the double helix structure of the DNA molecule that carries the genetic information to build a living being. Their findings opened up rich new fields of research in life sciences and medicine.

GREAT MINDS

Rosalind Franklin (1920–1958) was an English chemist working at King's College, London, in the 1950s. She made X-ray images of DNA that paved the way for Watson and Crick's discovery. She died before the importance of her work had been acknowledged.

GENETIC MAKEUP

Nearly all living organisms on Earth have DNA as their genetic material. The exceptions to this are some types of viruses, including the influenza and measles viruses. Instead, these viruses use a different molecule, which is called RNA (ribonucleic acid).

?
What is the Human Genome Project?

A full set of genes is called a "genome." The Human Genome Project was an international project that set out to map and understand our genes. A completed human genome sequence was published in 2003.

"A human must turn **information** into **intelligence** or **knowledge.**"

GRACE HOPPER

They called me "Amazing Grace," and I won't argue with that! Having studied math at Vassar and Yale, I worked at Harvard when America went to war in 1941. Employed by the Navy, I worked on the Mark 1 computer. Nothing like today's machines, the Mark 1 filled an entire room and was fed information using a paper tape with holes punched in it. It was love at first sight!

Computers for the Everyday

I was one of the first-ever computer programmers and I never wanted to do anything else. After the war, it became obvious (to me at least) that computers needed to be easy to operate if ordinary people were going to use them. I set about writing programs that allowed commands to be written in plain old English, instead of using alien-looking math symbols.

I helped develop the first programming languages that could work on many different computers and encouraged people to adopt these strange new machines. "We've always done things like this," they would say. "Yes, but look to the future, not to the past," I'd reply. And what a bright future it was!

TIME LINE

1906 Born in New York City

1944 Programs computers for the Navy at Harvard

1949 Works on the first commercial computer, UNIVAC 1

1959 Helps launch the COBOL programming language

1992 Dies in Arlington, Virginia

LEGACY

Grace Hopper was a distinguished mathematician and computer scientist. She played a leading role in the early development of programming languages and in making computers user-friendly for businesses and individuals.

ALARMING CHILD

When Grace Hopper was a seven-year-old, she decided to find out how an alarm clock worked by dismantling every clock in her family home. Her startled mother had to limit little Grace to one clock only.

BUGS AND GLITCHES

In 1947, Hopper's computer stopped functioning because a moth had become trapped in the machine. After removing the moth, Hopper said the computer had been debugged — and so **debugging** became the word for sorting out any kind of computer glitch.

?
Which was the first computer?
People don't agree on this, because it depends what you mean by a computer. The Harvard Mark 1 probably doesn't really count, because it used a mix of electronics and mechanical systems. ENIAC, made in 1946, was the first electronic general-purpose computer.

COMPUTER FIRSTS

Among her greatest achievements, Hopper:

★ Created the first compiler, allowing computers to run programs.

★ Made the first user-friendly programming language, called FLOW-MATIC.

★ Advocated computer networks linked to common databases.

"All **life is linked** to the **earth** from which it came."

RACHEL CARSON

Raised on a small farm, a fascination with nature led me to study marine biology at college. I worked as a marine biologist after graduation but soon turned to writing. *The Sea Around Us*, my book about the richness of life in the oceans, wowed the nation.

Chemical Nightmare

Happy in my career, I was far from happy with what I saw happening in America. Scientists had invented chemical products to destroy insects that harmed crops or carried disease. Farmers sprayed these pesticides across the countryside with little thought for the consequences. I realized something terrible was happening: The chemicals that took out fire ants and moths also killed blackbirds and meadowlarks. Perhaps more disturbing, the chemicals entered the food chain and ended up on our plates!

I put all my evidence into a book called *Silent Spring*. It caused a sensation and I was attacked by those making money from pesticides. I didn't mind — I was persuading millions of ordinary people to start caring about the damage humans were causing to the natural environment.

TIME LINE

1907 Born in Springdale, Pennsylvania

1936 Works as aquatic biologist at US Bureau of Fisheries

1951 Publishes *The Sea Around Us*

1962 Her influential book *Silent Spring* appears

1964 Dies in Silver Spring, Maryland

BYE-BYE BLACKBIRD

Carson called her famous book *Silent Spring* because she noticed that she no longer heard any birdsong at that time of year. She argued that this linked directly to the use of chemical sprays, which were poisoning the songbirds.

ENVIRONMENTAL MILESTONES

The publication of *Silent Spring* in 1962 prompted the following events:

★ **1970:** The US Environmental Protection Agency was formed.

★ **1972:** The first world conference on the environment was held in Stockholm, Sweden.

★ **1992:** The first UN-organized Earth Summit was held in Rio de Janeiro, Brazil.

LEGACY

American biologist Rachel Carson triggered the modern environmental movement in the United States with her book *Silent Spring*. Her work encouraged respect for nature and criticized the impact of chemicals on the environment.

DDT BANNED

Dichlorodiphenyltrichloroethane (DDT to you) was one of the main pesticides targeted by Carson's warnings. Its use was limited across the world during the decade that followed Carson's death. In the United States its agricultural use was banned altogether in 1972.

?

Did Carson call for a ban on pesticides?
Rachel Carson did not say that all use of chemicals for destroying harmful pests was wrong. She called for the use of pesticides to be reduced, with careful consideration given to their possible side effects.

"[We] are **not** the **only beings** with personalities . . . and emotions like **joy** and **sorrow**."

JANE GOODALL

I loved animals as a child but could never have guessed they'd become my life's work. Traveling to Africa in my twenties, I met anthropologist Louis Leakey. He was investigating human evolution and needed a researcher to study chimpanzees in their natural environment, and he picked me! I lived for long periods in the jungle, just me and the chimps. Eventually, they accepted me into their lives.

My Friends in the Wild
Over many years, I found that each chimp had its own personality, emotions, intelligence, and relationships. Up till then, scientists studying apes had given them numbers, but I preferred names like David Greybeard, Flo, and Humphrey. Well, why not? I showed that chimps were very much like humans socially, and that they could even make and use simple tools — things that had never been considered before my time.

Eventually, my life with the chimps went global and people learned about me through books and on TV. It seemed right that I should become a campaigner for the protection of apes and their environment. These animals were my friends, after all.

TIME LINE

1934 Born in London, England

1957 Meets anthropologist Louis Leakey in Kenya

1960 Begins studying chimpanzees at Gombe Stream in Tanzania

1971 Publishes book *In the Shadow of Man*

1977 Establishes the Jane Goodall Institute

LEGACY
Jane Goodall has studied chimpanzee families in the wild for more than fifty years. Her work has transformed our understanding of their behavior. Today, Goodall is a leading campaigner for conservation and animal rights.

GREAT MINDS
British-born **Louis and Mary Leakey** (1903–1972) and 1913–1996) were a husband-and-wife anthropological team. They studied fossils of early humans and human ancestors in Olduvai Gorge in eastern Africa, now Tanzania. It was thanks to their skull discoveries that Africa first became recognized as the home of the first humans.

FEISTY CREATURES
One of Goodall's most striking discoveries was that chimpanzees are not always peaceful vegetarians. She observed that they sometimes hunt and eat other animals. They also kill their own kind in disputes over territory and status — just like humans do.

❓
How smart are chimpanzees?
Jane Goodall showed that chimps use tools. For example, they fish termites out of holes using grass stalks. She also found they communicate with one another, using more than thirty different calls and a wide range of gestures and facial expressions.

DISTANT COUSINS
Biologists believe that humans are among the great apes, alongside chimpanzees, gorillas, and orangutans. All of these groups descend from one common ancestor. Chimpanzees and bonobos are the closest living relatives to humans and share many similarities in their DNA.

"My **goal** is simple. It is a **complete understanding** of the **universe** . . ."

STEPHEN HAWKING

Two things have dominated my life: a fascination with the universe and a terrible illness. While studying at Cambridge University, England, I was diagnosed with ALS, a progressive paralysis that was expected to kill me within a couple of years. I won't lie — until then I'd been pretty lazy, but not anymore!

Universal Truths

I didn't die, as it happened, but became one of the world's leading thinkers in an area of physics and cosmology that was far beyond the grasp of most people's minds. I made new predictions about the nature of black holes and contributed to a growing understanding of the Big Bang with which our universe began.

Despite becoming almost completely paralyzed, the miracles of modern technology have allowed me to continue working and communicating for decades. It is a dream of mine to travel in space and I once visited the Kennedy Space Center in Florida. While there, I experienced weightlessness in a gravity-free environment, floating free of the wheelchair to which I am usually confined. It was out of this world!

TIME LINE

1942 Born in Oxford, England

1963 Diagnosed as having amyotrophic lateral sclerosis (ALS)

1974 Discovers Hawking radiation

1988 Publishes bestseller *A Brief History of Time*

BIG BANG THEORY

Many scientists believe that the universe began about fourteen billion years ago. The universe has been expanding from a single point, becoming cooler and less dense ever since. It is the start of this expansion that they call the **Big Bang**.

LEGACY

Stephen Hawking is a theoretical physicist. He uses math to explore the origins of the universe and the nature of black holes in space. He is best known as the author of *A Brief History of Time,* which explains his discoveries to the general public.

FAR OUT, MAN!

Hawking has said that:

* Time travel is perfectly possible, at least in theory.
* The colonization of space is essential, as Earth will become uninhabitable.
* Machines with artificial intelligence will pose a real threat to human life in the future.

INTO A BIG BLACK HOLE

The breakthrough idea that made Stephen Hawking's reputation as a physicist was that black holes emit radiation (a form of energy). This contradicted the previously accepted idea that nothing can escape a black hole. The energy is called **Hawking radiation** in Stephen's honor.

?

How does Hawking speak?
Stephen Hawking has not been able to speak naturally since 1985. He uses a device that allows him to select words on-screen, which are then spoken by a voice synthesizer. He currently operates the device using a cheek muscle.

"The **Web** does not just connect **machines**, it connects **people**."

TIM BERNERS-LEE

A computer software engineer during the 1980s, I was in my element. Computers were so new and exciting back then! I worked for a major scientific research center in Switzerland, called CERN. At the time, the Internet connected computer networks across the world, including ours, yet researchers in different countries still found it hard to communicate.

Going Hyper
I had the idea of using hypertext (text with links) to turn the Internet into a fully accessible global system for sharing information. Ambitious, I know!

I set up a system to serve the scientists at CERN, but, really, I had a vision that went far beyond the scientific community. I called it the World Wide Web. It was my dream to make the Web available to all — free in every sense, with no one controlling access or content, and no fees. To make this happen, I established a consortium at the MIT Laboratory of Computer Science in Cambridge.

Since then, my system has grown to immense proportions. Recently, I set up a foundation to ensure the Web fulfills its mission to benefit humanity across the globe. Dreams can come true!

TIME LINE

1955 Born in London, England

1980 Creates the first hypertext database system

1989 Invents the World Wide Web

1994 Founds the World Wide Web Consortium

2009 Establishes the World Wide Web Foundation

LEGACY

Tim Berners-Lee is the man who created the World Wide Web and did the most to make it a system that everyone could use. He continues to campaign to see his vision become reality — a world in which everyone is interconnected.

GREAT MINDS

The American computer experts **Bob Kahn** (b. 1938) and **Vint Cerf** (b. 1943) are often called the fathers of the Internet. They invented the basic protocols (rules for transmitting data) that allow computers all over the world to communicate with one another.

FREE FOR ALL

Tim Berners-Lee has long been a passionate supporter of **Net Neutrality**. This is the principle that the services of the Internet should be freely available to all users on an equal basis. Berners-Lee considers this principle to be under continual threat from various government and commercial pressures.

?

Aren't the Internet and the World Wide Web the same thing?
Not quite. The Internet is the network that connects millions of computers globally. The World Wide Web is a method of accessing and sharing information via the Internet. The Web is just one use of the Internet — e-mail, for example, is a separate system.

WORLD'S FIRST WEBSITE

On August 6, 1991, Tim Berners-Lee set up the first-ever website. Its address was **http://info.cern.ch**. Visitors to the site could read about the World Wide Web and how it worked. There was even information about setting up a website of one's own.

GLOSSARY

ALCHEMY An early unscientific type of chemistry, in which practitioners sought to turn ordinary metals into gold.

ALGEBRA A form of math that uses letters or symbols instead of numbers.

ANTIBIOTICS Medicines that attack bacteria.

ARITHMETIC A form of math that involves making calculations using numbers.

ASTROLOGY The belief that the positions of the sun, moon, stars, and planets influence people's characters and various aspects of their lives.

ATOM The tiniest part of an element that has all the properties of that element. A source of energy in nuclear power stations, atoms are also the explosive force in atom bombs.

BACTERIA Tiny living creatures that exist everywhere on Earth, including in the human body. Some bacteria cause illnesses, while others can be beneficial to a person's health.

BINARY CODE A way of representing any word or number using only two digits—0 and 1—or two states, on and off.

CATHOLIC A Christian who belongs to the Roman Catholic Church. The Roman Catholic Church is under the leadership of the Pope, who lives in Vatican City, Rome.

COMMUNIST Communism is a political system that was established in Russia and other countries during the twentieth century. It places the good of the group ahead of the good of the individual.

CONSTELLATION A group of stars as seen from Earth.

ECLIPSE A solar eclipse occurs when the moon blocks light from the sun. A lunar eclipse happens when the shadow of the earth falls across the moon.

ELEMENT In chemistry, an element is a pure substance consisting of a single type of atom.

ELLIPSE An oval shape, like a stretched circle.

EQUATION In math, a statement that two groups of numbers or symbols are equal.

ETHER An imaginary element once believed to fill outer space.

EVOLUTION The gradual change of animals and plants, creating new species over long periods of time.

EXILE Being banned from living in your native country, usually for political reasons.

FORCE FIELD The area across which a force such as gravity, magnetism, or electricity exerts its effect.

GALAXY A vast number of stars held together by gravity in a single system within the universe.

GENE A section of DNA that determines a single inherited characteristic such as eye color.

GENERATOR A mechanical device that generates an electric current.

GENETICS The study of how characteristics are inherited from one generation to the next in humans, animals, and plants.

GEOLOGY The scientific study of the earth, including rocks, earthquakes, and volcanoes.

GEOMETRY The branch of math that deals with lines and shapes — for example, triangles, squares, circles, and cubes.

GRAVITY The force of attraction that holds planets in orbit around the sun and makes objects fall toward the center of the earth.